Where Now

Also by Laura Kasischke

Laura Kasischke

Where Now

New and Selected Poems

Copper Canyon Press
Port Townsend, Washington

Cover art: Natacha Nikouline, Series: *In Situ*, Title: *Lac St Cassein*, 2015.

Copper Canyon Press is in residence at Fort Worden State Park in Port Townsend, Washington, under the auspices of Centrum. Centrum is a gathering place for artists and creative thinkers from around the world, students of all ages and backgrounds, and audiences seeking extraordinary cultural enrichment.

LIBRARY OF CONGRESS CATALOGING-IN-PUBLICATION DATA
Names: Kasischke, Laura, 1961- author.
Title: Where now : new and selected poems / Laura Kasischke.
Description: Port Townsend, Washington : Copper Canyon Press, [2017]
Identifiers: LCCN 2016055771 (print) | LCCN 2017001966 (ebook) | ISBN
    9781556595127 (hardcover) 9781556596445 (paperback) | ISBN 9781619321724 (E-book)
Subjects: | BISAC: POETRY / American / General.
Classification: LCC PS3561.A6993 A6 2017 (print) | LCC PS3561.A6993 (ebook) |
    DDC 811/.54--dc23
LC record available at https://lccn.loc.gov/2016055771

Copper Canyon Press
Post Office Box 271
Port Townsend, Washington 98368

www.coppercanyonpress.org

for Bill

Hwær cwom mearg? Hwær cwom mago?
Hwær cwom maþþumgyfa?
Hwær cwom symbla gesetu?
Hwær sindon seledreamas?
Eala beorht bune!
Eala byrnwiga!
Eala þeodnes þrym!
Hu seo þrag gewat,
genap under nihthelm,
swa heo no wære.

from "The Wanderer," anon.

IG-88, WHERE R U?

Boba Fett and the Assassin Droids

Contents

THREE

from *Space, in Chains*

FOUR

from *Lilies Without*

FIVE

from *Gardening in the Dark*

SIX

from *Dance and Disappear*

SEVEN

from *Fire & Flower*

TEN

from *Wild Brides*

ELEVEN

New Poems

Where Now

Their holiness, their loneliness, the song
they sing in certain barns
on sad, old farms ·
about the scales on which the love
was weighed, or the terrible
armchair onto which was tossed
a small girl's nightgown once. The
widower's broken ankle, and the summer
a transparent fish was caught
in the pond. Invisible if not
for its heart. Its lungs. The throbbing
jelly of its subconscious:
No one would fry it for supper.
Like Dora, Little Hans, the Rat Man.
When Freud told them their own secrets
surely they must have asked, "But,
Herr Doctor, how do you know?"
And these owls in the rafters urging
me all winter now to *Go,*
go, and throw
your mother's bones behind you as you go.

ONE

New Poems

Where is the horse? Where the rider?

Ubi sunt?

In the mirror, like something strangled by an angel — this
woman glimpsed much later, still

wearing her hospital gown. Behind her — mirrors, and
more mirrors, and, in them, more cold faces. Then

the knocking, the pounding — all of them wanting to be
let out, let in. The one-way conversations. Mostly not

anything to worry about, really. Mild accusations, merely.
Never actual threats. (Anyway, what could they possibly

do to you now from inside their locked, glass places?)
Still, some innocent question on some special occasion

might bring it all back to you again, such as: *Might
you simply have forgotten where you left me when you left me?*

Or — *Shouldn't you be searching all the harder for me then?*
Or — the question that might frighten any woman being

asked this of her own reflection (no
tears on its face, a smile instead) — *How far*

did you really think I'd go without you? Then —
Don't you think that's where you'll find us now?

The Whole

The surgeon peels the man
away from the man
to get a look at the whole
throbbing thing of him. The slick

little change-purses, the seaweed. His
featherless birds
moistly dreaming. The rubied globes, but also
the mossy blades and edges. The rotting branches hanging
low with soggy leaves. And then

one velvet tail curled around a pulp-pink stone, right
next to the fetal totalitarians, their shallow breathing. The sticky
eyelids of a forgotten kitten. And that girl at Woodstock — too
young to be there, it seemed — lost

in the rainstorm in the dark among the demons, so that
the faster she ran the faster the tentacles sprang
out of the mud to snag her ankles. Her

skinny thighs, slippery with blood and spit. The rose

bloated in the bowl at the center of the great-aunt's table.
A cockroach crushed beneath the bridegroom's heel.
A pearl fallen off the wedding dress, swallowed by a baby girl.
The stippled button, snipped from the suit coat of the eldest
son in his coffin, pocketed by his brother. Then

the shameful, rubbery secret at the center of all of us, which
for this man long since slipped into the gut of an iridescent
fish (faceless) floating
here now in this thickened ocean between
today's patient's gray-eyed tumor (eyelashed, blushing) and
his liver, mucus-gleaming. The whole of it

just trying to be polite. As when
the in-laws would arrive on Sunday mornings, unannounced, in
their church clothes at one o'clock in the afternoon while we
were still sleeping off the night before. The door

opening very wide ("Hi!") as if none of it
had come as a surprise. Because

nature simply couldn't figure out another way
to make us, frankly, there being
so many things that no one wants to see.
The gallbladder, for instance. The spleen. The

intestines gathered as
a sodden bouquet of carnations some days, and
a roiling nest of shining snakes on other days. Or

the cook in the kitchen pinching the skin off the surface
of the scalded hollandaise
with his filthy fingernails.

Oh, the waitress knows, and ladles the sauce over
your eggs Benedict anyway. And
the surgeon knows.
Sews you closed.

Disasters Involving Dictionaries

Men and women behind iron bars.

How freedom always arrives
with the jangling of keys. But we

played other games as children, didn't we?

Besides Captivity, there was
Machine. And God spoke to us
in limericks and in dreams. And

now and then an angry teacher
chased us down the staircase, bearing
a dictionary. *This*

will teach you to mess around with —

Then she used a word we'd
never heard before, and haven't since —

although it clearly had some meaning.

Like a dog darting into traffic, chasing a rat.
And the pileup after that — but

no one's injured, no one's killed. Just
a few insurance claims, a bit of auto-
body damage, and

that dog, defeated but alive — wet, red mouth
open wide, drinking in the summer breeze
of having been granted a second life, and

all the extra attention that comes with that.

He loved me, I guess, that boy. Whole

seasons he spent pawing like a fox
at the fence around the chicken house. (*No* —

she isn't home. Go away. Laura's in the bathtub.
She can never come to the phone.) But

why could I not love him back? Perhaps

everything I was then was
dried cement? Or

maybe all my branches had been broken
off by then, or they were in the process
of being broken already by all the things I
loved so much more than I could ever
have loved him?

Now, to be a stranger in a grave-
yard, and to understand that — given

the dates they'll chisel on my own
stone one day — I, too, was one of those
millions of children who sat, cross-
legged on the floor in front of a television set
to watch as our astronauts planted, on
our moon, our flag   Yes:

I had to have been witness to
this, my era's most significant event. So —
why can't I remember
anything about it?

Like the worm on its way to the center of the cabbage:
A crisis at the core of certain things.
Loves that couldn't last. The boy in Spain. The death-

row pen pal. The old
woman walking straight into the mirror, and then
rubbing her eyes, backing up, trying it again.

We all cried, *Stop!* but she kept walking.

And you were warned that it would be
a happy song followed by a brutal fact.
Eagle-headed god forged out of gold. A rag stuffed into a human hole.
My young son at the planetarium, and how
he asked me when they turned the lights back on,
"Are we on Earth again
now, Mom?" To end it all
on the universe's terms.

Or not:
Needleful
of pentobarbital.
And the cat, the cat, our last
green and peaceful gaze after
a lifetime of that. How, after that, in my arms, the

planet's bonds slackened.

To have reached the source of all that sweetness.
That satisfaction.
No turning back.

Who would turn back?

Once, I was as large
as any living creature could be.

I could lift the world and carry it
from my breast to its bath.

When I looked down from the sky
you could see the love in my eye:

"O tiny world, if anything
ever happened to you, I would die."

And I said, "No!" to the hand. Snatched
the pebble from the mouth, fished it out

and told the world it would choke!
Warned the world over & over! "Do

you hear me? Do you want to choke?!"

But how was the world to know
what the truth might be? *Perhaps*

they grant you special powers, these
choking stones. Maybe

they change the child into a god, all-swallowing.

For, clearly, there *were* other gods.
The world could see

that I, too, was at the mercy of something.
Sure, I could point to the sky

and say its name, but I couldn't make it change.
Some days it was blue, true, but others

were ruined by its gray:
"I'm sorry, little world —

no picnic, no parade, no swimming pool today…"

And the skinned knee in spite of me.
And *why else would there be*

such terror in the way she screamed, and the horn honking,
and the squealing wheels, and, afterward, her cold

sweat against my cheek?

Ah, she wants us to live forever.
It's her weakness… Now I see!

But, once, I was larger
than any other being —

larger, perhaps, than any being
had any right to be.

Because, of course, eventually, the world
grew larger, and larger, until it could lift

me up and put me down anywhere
it pleased. Until, finally, I would need

its help to move the birdbath, the book-
shelf, the filing cabinet. "And

could you put my desk by the window, sweetie?"

A truck, two men, one of them my son, and
everything I ever owned, and they

didn't even want to stop for lunch.

Even the freezer. Even the piano.
("If you can move it you can have it.")

But, once, I swear, I was… And now
this trunk in the attic to prove it:

These shoes in the palm of my hand?
You used to wear them on your feet.

This blanket the size of a hand towel?
I used wrap it around you sleeping

in my arms like this. See? This
is how small the world used to be when

everything else in the world was me.

Pandora's Cellar

Who canned her summer peaches
in her own tears. Fruit

made of daylight, shelved
in a cellar for thirty years.

We found those jars
along with all
the other things she'd hidden —
wearing yellowed dresses —
after she was dead. That

morning, distant thunder, followed
by a downpour. The lights went

out. They came back on again.

"Dear God," my mother said, turning
around to find me with a mason jar

flashing in my hands. "Do
not take the lid off of that thing, Laura."

But I did. Of course. I had.

Shadow

The shadow says, "Inside my head, just
shadow, and more shadow, but with

substance, more or less, or
so I wish to believe of myself." So—

shadow thoughts then? Shadow
memories? And
what regrets might shadows have?

Well, I suppose, it's all just shadow then.
Restless, all of it, all of it ocean, perhaps—

a body of water full of fish, and full of the way
fish slip below the surface, like—well, like

shadows, which are suggestions, except—

What about whales then? My God! Whales—

drunken whales on drunken waves. Like tragic fates.
Like public humiliations. Like the kinds of mistakes
that get written about on the Internet these days, and
stay there forever in cyberspace. Or—

worse, the kinds of things that make the local papers
along with your address and your name. So that

these are no longer shadows, it seems. These
are solidities, chained to your wrists, stapled
to your feet, as you

blunder forward clumsily, backward
gracefully — but, also, as
previously established, without

weight, not even the weight of the mind, which
is sloppy, too, and tends to splash
all over the place, while also managing to be

the dense and bloody brick
containing everything, as
we move in and out of conversations
with total strangers, or tune our
radios into certain stations, while

standing in the sun, or beneath the streetlamp, or
you rise up in a classroom — innocently enough —

from your desk one afternoon, until
you're standing between
the dust-warm light as it pours
forth from the projector onto the screen

so that all the other students (who've
been watching, in their trances, a battleship
crossing the Atlantic, headed toward something
awful in the past) are shouting at you now:

"For God's sake sit down!"

While you, confused, glance around, with no
idea your shadow was a passenger on that.

The Breath

There is a butcher who is also the shepherd.

Some things were promised, but others were not.

The first breath feeds, apparently, the tiny
lily inside the baby. But
the second is your father hauling that
sled up the hill again. And

all the breaths in between
this one and the last. A tale
frantically whispered
to a child — the moral of which is *To live.*

So that the clay breathes beside the pond in August.
And the apples on the branches breathe in fall.
The deer's nostrils. The nostrils of a goddess. My

grandfather coughing himself to death in the back
bedroom of 1976, with the sound of children

sharpening sticks. And my mother's final
gasp as well — as if
just then she had to witness it again:

her only daughter on her way
to the back door, bearing a bouquet
made of all the flowers in the neighbor's garden.
And how her final breath sounded

just like that screen door, opening fast.

The Hourglass

I take a little detour off the freeway now and then
to get a glimpse of their
high celestial shine again —

the guard towers and the razor wire and the silvery cement
of the prison where my cousin Kenny lived (felonious
assault/armed robbery) for
seven years until he was set free, and married, bought
a house out in the country, where he lived
another seven
years happily (it seemed)

until one day he took a chainsaw to a tree
to rid his property of some tree disease, and in
the course of this was pinned beneath
a limb so heavy that it took
four men to lift it off of him. He

was dead already when they found him, so
no one knows how long he might have
borne that weight and lingered — whether
it took him many hours to die, or if, as they

so often say, he never knew what hit him.

But long before this end, my
cousin would ride his bike ten miles across forbidden
busy streets on Saturdays to play with me a game
we called Don't Kill Me, Kenny, Please.

Because to say this was the only way to win.

It was the kind of play that made my parents
wary, so when

we heard my father's pockets full of keys, we
turned on the TV and pretended to be watching:

The laughter, meaningless.
The hijinks and the wasted drama, completely
wasted on the likes of him and me, while
the hourglass of the living room seemed to be
so stuffed with sand it never budged. How

could it? Tedium, being — as we
would both learn better, later, in our
very different ways — the highest
of all the prices to be paid for
getting in or staying out of trouble.

Until one day, despite the parents
everywhere, he got a knife out of the kitchen, and
chased me with it to the toolshed, where
I was supposed to say, "Don't kill
me, Kenny, please." But didn't. I just
stood there, instead, understanding

how weary one might grow of games like this—
(although, in truth, I wasn't weary yet). I lifted
my shirt, pointed to my heart, said, "Go ahead."

Well, of course, he didn't. He
rolled his eyes, tossed his
knife to the floor of the shed, and then, sounding

to me like a very old man (older, as it
turned out, than
he would ever be) and
also (more surprisingly) as if, perhaps he'd
already considered that possibility
regardless of what I said, and he

told me he was sorry, but this wasn't something he
was willing to go to prison for—killing
his stupid cousin, who was also boring. So

I said: "Don't kill me, Kenny."
(Sigh.)
"Please."

Of course, I wanted to live, mostly, but maybe I
also had some sense already of my-

self driving like this one day
past all the brilliant sprawl of all the time ahead, feeling

as if I'd already escaped my life without regrets. Or
might. And maybe I

even got a glimpse of all those prisoners
(they're out there once in a while)
shuffling around on the other side
of an electric fence — which

would have been humming, even then, in
my subconscious, in
the sun.

The Enormous Cage

She said, I have a dirty little secret
to tell you. It

will explain everything. And then

she blew it into the beak
of a very tiny bird
in an enormous cage. The

bird, of course, slipped
through the bars and flew away:

What they took with them when they died.
What they almost said but wouldn't say.
Now, one or two on almost
every branch
nearly every sunny day. And

also on the phone lines, even
in the rain. Also, some
nights I feel its miniature

feet tread my spine, then sink in
between my shoulder blades, as if

its dirty little wings were also mine.

The Wall

One night from the other side
of a motel wall made of nothing but
sawdust and pink stuff, I

listened as a man cried
to someone on the telephone
that all he wanted
to do before he died
was to come home.

"I want to come home!"

That night a man cried
until I was ankle-deep in sleep,
and then up to my neck, wading
like a swimmer
or like a suicide
through the waves
of his crying
and into the deep

as icebergs cracked into halves
as jellyfish, like thoughts, were
passed secretly between people.

And the seaweed, like
the sinuous soft green hair
of certain beauty queens
washed up by the sea.
Except that we

were in Utah, and one of us
was weeping

while the other one
was sleeping, with

nothing but a thin, dry
wall between us.

For the Return of the Bee

after Bill Abernethy's translation of the Old English charm

Repeat, repeat, repeat:

Lord Christ, where is our bee?
She who stole the sugar bowl, sucked
lingeringly from the pink rose every spring, licked
the sticky bottom of the brandy snifter clean?

You shall not escape me, nor ever be free of me.

The way our words linger now forever in the ether.
Just try to snatch back a single
one of your own little secrets.
Once, I tried, and my
fingers glittered for a minute against the computer screen.
Then, nothing, permanently.

Return, return, return to me.

Even a can of frosting from the pantry.
Even the Sweet 'n Lo packets beneath the sink.

Surely, she who was its source could not also be its thief.

So, where can she be hiding now that nothing
disappears, or goes unheard, unseen. For we

can listen to our enemies whispering on mountain peaks.
We can place a target on the heart of any
anarchist, Imam, member of the Tea Party, and
even through the deep

privacy of the sea

we can send a wave of electricity
smooth as a memory.
And I myself have witnessed

a miracle as it was happening:

a child in the backseat
of a car in a parking lot behind a bar
waiting for his father in the middle of the night, while

the whole thing was being filmed
by a satellite from the sky
by what that child must have believed
to be a star.

My Father's Stoicism

First
I'm wearing a dark gown
too long to walk in, so I must
sit down on the ground
and hack the bottom of it off.

Second
I offer my father a cup of coffee
which he drinks
standing up.

Third
I begin to suspect there is a cave
beneath my house
and it connects me
to this place.

Fourth
I see that peacock
in agony.

Fourth
I see that peacock
in agony
again
in the doorway
with his dead arm dangling
and a cigarette
and no one to light it
while we all sit
at a table
and chew
the pages of our soup
while Alexandria

burns to the ground
except for the library
in flames in his brain
and all the words he
never wrote down
and would never say.

The Widows' Neighborhood

The houses are like crooked teeth, all
up and down this street. A man's
empty shirt dances, electrocuted
on a laundry line. In

broad daylight, garbage cans full
of flies, and three old wives with only
one old husband
between them. They

call him
Silence, and take turns slicing
his meat
into such thin pieces
he doesn't even
know he's eating.

In the garden, a mandrake
has been planted. The root
of it, of course, is

shaped like a little man. Being

pulled out of the ground, it
shrieks — and this sound
is always followed

by the arrival
of an unexpected wolf, or lion.

What I Learned in Ninth Grade

Always, it's early winter, and you can always
see through the venetian blinds
that you are floating, and lost
in a classroom made of mist. And that

the false flattery of certain groups of girls
is a feast of pure sugar that you must eat
with your eyes closed while you
swallow down its spoonfuls
along with your flatterers' smiles.

And you'll do it. Tropism =

a natural inclination. The roots
grow down. The bird flies up. In some
future my husband will run toward the accident
to see whether we can help, while I'll stand
frozen on the sidewalk
covering my eyes with my hands.

But that was just Biology.
And Mrs. Anders liked me. Elsewhere

there's a number
that is not the phone number of a friend, but
which I'm told I have to memorize, for

without this number, the whole
civilization will have to end, and I might
never go on to tenth grade, remaining
forever in ninth.

God, how hard Mr. Nestor was trying
in his raging kindness and shiny ties

to teach us what it meant
to designate the ratio of the circumference of
a circle to its diameter, and to call it *pi*.

But this was Dummy Math. Some of us
were sleeping. Some of us were high.
Some of us were so desperate and confused
that we were weeping. Surely

he wasn't serious. We
would never flunk or die. Surely
one day a cure could be found for the kind
of cancer my mother had, and
then there would no longer be
this need for math. Surely

some researcher at some place
like Harvard — a place
I've been assured
I'll never see — will
discover this eventually. And even

if a cure for math cannot be found, can
math not simply be destroyed? This

is the greatest country in the world. Why
must its children suffer under *pi*? Cannot

a scapegoat be slaughtered on an altar
as in the Bible? Or an entire
civilization, as in the past? May we

not bomb it, invade it, steal its oil —
or set its oil wells on fire at least? To

my fellow soldiers (dummies, all of us
— ruthless, and proud of it) I

said, "We will spare their children
if we can, of course, but
only if they renounce their god of *pi*…"

Yes, in another year I would learn of love
from reading about Daisy and Jay. But
in ninth grade I learned about hatred: How

to raise an army in my imagination.
How to dress it in bright uniforms
with hierarchical stripes. How
to spray the peaceful valleys of my
enemies with pesticides
until it rained poisonous butterflies onto
their flesh from the skies. And then, sweet

Jesus, after it had already been
memorized, to be told
that 3.14159
is not quite *pi*.

Because *pi* is irrational,
and transcendent, so
pi might just go on and on.

Or not go on.

Like ninth grade, or civilization, which
also began
and ended in Babylon.

The Sound of Icicles Broken Off the Eaves

with a broomstick — shattering and glassy, all daggers and plans, while

the woman in the wheelchair across the hall from my
father's room in the nursing home struggled all day to untangle
an invisible ball of string, or

some other endlessly tangled thing. "Mother!" she called out each time

she caught a glimpse of me — and then she'd hold it up, pleadingly. The nurses
　　　　and the aides would watch this scene from behind their
desks, behind their eyes, so that I, too, had to pretend to be surprised —

(*She never says a word to anyone but you...*)

and gave her my falsest little smile, patted her head, as if I didn't know
perfectly well what knot it was she'd been trying all her life
to unknot for me, for
my salvation, as

if I didn't recognize
her — my only child.

TWO

from *The Infinitesimals*

Where the giver of treasure?

Binoculars

This bird on the other side
of my binoculars — the cold life-light
around its mind, which was never
meant to be seen this clearly by a human being.
Still standing, decades later, in
a corridor, crying, having run from the room unable
to watch my mother die:
So there she is instead for the rest of my life. This
bird (my husband says it is a *flicker*) pretending
not to be staring straight back into my eye.

The Second Trumpet

One day in August I went
to the lobby of the hospital to listen.
One icy night in February
I drove my car into a ditch.
Once, I saw a dog in traffic, and then

the child running after it.

And after the funeral.
And just before the diagnosis.
And when
the phone call did not come
but I did not yet know what that meant.

Each time, expecting trumpets, I
received silence instead.
Expecting angels, tongues
on a slaughterhouse floor. At
the bottom of a filthy cage, their
feathers, silence, and a smell

like a classroom full of children's
sweaters, but which
might have been adrenaline.
Something glandular.
Something chemical.

It always lasted
half an hour, and then —

At the End of the Text, a Small Bestial Form

This is the glimpse of the god you were never supposed to get.
Like the fox slipping into the thicket.
Like the thief in the night outside the window. The cool
gray dorsal fin in the distance. Invisible
mountain briefly visible through the mist
formed of love and guilt.

And the stranger's face hidden in the family picture. The one

imagining her freedom, like

the butterfly blown against the fence
in her best yellow dress
by the softest breeze of summer:

To have loved
and to have suffered. To have waited
for nothing, and for nothing to have come.

And the water like sleek black fur combed back that afternoon:

The young lovers rowed a boat. The boy
reeled in a fish. The husband
smiled, raising
a toast.

While the children grew anxious
for dinner. While something
struggled under the water,
bound by ropes.
And the warm milk dribbled down the sick man's chin.
And the wife, the mother, the daughter, the hostess, and those
few people on Earth she would ever wish were dead
were the ones she loved the most.

Mushrooms

Like silent naked monks huddled
around an old tree stump, having
spun themselves in the night
out of thought and nothingness —

And God so pleased with their silence
He grants them teeth and tongues.

Like us.

How long have you been gone?
A child's hot tears on my bare arms.

This Is Not a Poem/Fairy Tale

Sixteen years ago in northern Michigan, somewhere in the Huron National Forest, a man and a woman from a nearby town pulled over to the shoulder of the road, took their two-year-old son, asleep, out of the backseat, walked with him into the woods a mile or so, and set him down.

It was still light enough for them to find their way back to their car. God help us, they went home.

These people. Drugs were involved, we must suppose. Some kind of profound stupidity made greater with desperation. (Although it isn't possible to have sympathy for them, one still searches for some explanation.)

Did they sleep that night? Were they startled when the phone at the bedside rang?

Well, they confessed the whole thing the next day after the child was found walking ("toddling," the finder called it) along that shoulder of the road. A policeman recognized him from his own child's day-care center. And he was a "smart little guy. He knew his name." This much was in the paper.

Everything else you have to imagine for yourself in order to survive, as he did. In order to survive it, you have to imagine it every day. When you lie down to go to sleep, and when you wake. But, in between —

In between, your mind is full of trees.
And it's quite dark despite the moon.
But this summer's been a warm one.
And someone tied your tiny shoes for you.

Small boy running through the center of the park, un-
zipping summer straight down the middle as he runs until
all the small boys come tumbling out. All

the small boys pouring from the world's fissure into
the world: My

father with a ball and bat. My
husband with a wooden gun. My son in
a cowboy hat. Their
shaving creams and razors. Their

little shoes.
Their untied laces. While

a woman, always younger, behind them in a sundress
calls their names, at first so sweetly
before she's angry — and then
in panic:

Come back, come back. She'll have

a few sharp words to share if she can ever catch them — although
she knows also there will never, never, never be
any time for that. Those

boys continuing to run. Their
trembling chins. Their
little feet I loved and loved, and
would kiss again and again.

You've Come Back to Me

for G

A small thing crawling toward me
across this dark lawn. Bright
eyes the only thing I'm sure I see.

You've come back to me,
haven't you, my sweet? From
long ago, and very far. Through

crawling dark, my sweet, you've
come back to me, have you? Even
smaller this time than the stars.

The Common Cold

To me she arrives this morning
dressed in some
man's homely, soft, cast-off
lover's shawl, and some
woman's memory of a third-
grade teacher
who loved her students a little too much.
(Those warm hugs that went
on and on and on.)

She puts her hand to my head and says,
"Laura, you should go back to bed."

But I have lunches to pack, socks
on the floor, while
the dust settles on
the *I've got to clean this pigsty up.*
(Rain at a bus stop.
Laundry in a closet.)

And tonight I'm
the Athletic Booster mother
whether I feel like it or not, weakly

taking your dollar
from inside my concession stand:

I offer you your caramel corn. (Birdsong
in a terrarium. Some wavering distant
planet reflected in a puddle.)

And, as your dollar
passes between us, perhaps
you will recall

how, years ago, we
flirted over some impossible
Cub Scout project.
Hammers

and saws, and seven
small boys tossing
humid marshmallows
at one another. And now

those sons, taller
and faster than we are, see
how they are poised on a line, ready
to run at the firing of a gun?

But here we are again, you and I, the
two of us tangled up
and biological: I've

forgotten your name, and
you never knew mine, but
in the morning
you'll find

my damp kisses all over your pillows,
my clammy flowers
blooming in your cellar,
my spring grass
dewed with mucus —

and you'll remember me
and how, tonight, wearing my
Go Dawgs T-shirt, I

stood at the center
of the sweet clinging heat
of a concession stand
with my flushed cheeks, and

how, before we touched, I
coughed into my hand.
Look:

here we are together
in bed all day again.

May Morning

The thoughts of the schoolgirl dragging
her backpack across the grass.
The thoughts of the sleep-
walker, and the trashman, and
the flower tender, and the
teenage couple at the mall.

Like I have been handed them all.
Like I have heard their music, as

if the saints. The way
the lilacs that day. As if

a glass box of it. Like

a vial of perfume poured all
over the whole of creation —
perfume extracted from the sky.
Like no grammar.
No makeup.
No time behind my blindfold:

When the hospitalized child
stopped me in the hallway
and told me his name.
Sebastian.

His little white gown. His tiny smile. Blind-
fold yanked off after thousands of years.

Who needed eyes?

Our rooster's name is Ivan.
He rules the world.
He stands on a bucket to assist
the sun in its path
through the sky. He
will not be attending
the funeral, for God

has said to Ivan, *You*
will never be sick
or senile. I'll
kill you with lightning
or let you drown. Or

I'll simply send
an eagle down
to fetch you when you're done.

So Ivan stands on a bucket
and looks around:

Human
stupidity.
The pitiful
cornflakes in their bowls.
The statues of their fascists.
The insane division of their cells.
The misinterpretations
of their bibles. Their
homely combs — and,

today, absurdly, their
crisp black clothes.

But Ivan keeps his thoughts
to himself, and crows.

It is a cow standing there in that field
at the center of this meteor shower.
My father's teeth in a dish, and a little
jewelry box with a bit
of lightning in it. Closed lid. The future
movie star glimpsed
from the subway tracks by a rat. Wrist-
watch on a sunken ship on the captain's
wrist. The shining
nakedness inside
her gown
of the bride. At the bottom
of the watery cave, a single
neon fish. Such

stillness.
Complete.
And you, with
your head on a satin pillow in a box as they
wheeled you out of the church
(I watched it)
into the parking lot
(from my car).

Perspective

Like the lake turned to
steel by the twilit
sky. Like
the Flood in the toilet
to the housefly.
Like the sheet
thrown over

the secret love. Like
the sheet thrown over
the blood on the rug.

Or the pages
of the novel
scattered by the wind:
the end
at the beginning
in the middle again.

And the sudden sense.
The polished lens.
The revision
revisioned, as if
as if.

As if
the secret —
had you told me when:
who I thought
we were, every-
where we went.

Door

Broken door this morning
banging in the wind, like
someone who slammed it once
and stomped away
and wanted to be let back in:

Memory, and
longing, but
not this morning.

Not this morning, as I

lie unburdened in the
creeping sun, and think *Thank
God* my father is two years ashes, and
my mother is so long and safely
dead and gone. All

over, all
over, their
embryonic unfolding, the
slow brass clock on their mantel, the
peaches they liked to savor in summer.

And our family jokes, our
secret passwords, their
hopeful faces, their
corn on the cob and their paper plates.

Thank God. *Thank God.*
Buried, burned, forgotten
where nothing else can harm them.

For the Young Woman I Saw Hit by a Car While Riding Her Bike

I'll tell you up front: She was fine — although
she left in an ambulance because
I called 9-1-1

and what else can you do
when they've come for you
with their sirens and lights
and you're young and polite
except get into their ambulance
and pretend to smile?

"Thanks," she said to me
before they closed her up. (They

even tucked
her bike in there. Not
one bent spoke on either tire.) But I

was shaking and sobbing too hard to say goodbye.

I imagine her telling her friends later, "It

hardly grazed me, but
this lady who saw it went crazy…"

I did. I was
molecular, while
even the driver who hit her did
little more than roll his eyes, while

a trucker stuck at the intersection, wolfing
down a swan
sandwich behind the wheel, sighed. Some-

one touched me on the shoulder
and asked, "Are you all right?"

(Over
in ten seconds. She
stood, all
blond, shook
her wings like a little cough.)

"Are you
okay?" someone else asked me. Uneasily. As if

overhearing my heartbeat
and embarrassed for me
that I was made
of such gushing meat
in the middle of the day
on a quiet street.

"They should have put *her*
in the ambulance, not me."

Laughter.
Shit happens.
To be young.
To shrug it off:

But, ah, sweet
thing, take
pity. One

day you too may be
an accumulation
of regrets, catastrophes.
A clay animation
of Psalm 73 (*But*

as for me, my feet…). No. It will be
Psalm 48: *They*

saw it,
and so they marveled; they
were troubled, and hasted away. Today

you don't remember the way
you called my name, so
desperately, a thousand times, tearing

your hair, and your clothes on the floor, and
the nurse who denied your morphine
so that you had to die that morning
under a single sheet
without me, in
agony, but

this time I was beside you.
I waited, and I saved you.
I was there.

A tail, a torso, a tiny face.
A longing, a journey, a deep belief.
A spawning, a fissioning, a bit of tissue
anchored to a psyche,
stitched to a wish.
Watery. Irony. Memory. My
mother, my face, and then

the last thing
she'd ever see, and then
the last words
I'd hear her say: *You're
killing me.*

Milk Tree

Heavy fruit
on bony branches
full of the knowledge one always encounters
too late
at the end of a life. Some

aspirin mixed with water, and a mouse
born in a dream. The sounds my son
once made while suckling. That, made
manifest. Little
milksop
and myself. Our

bodies, temporary
shelters, rented
breath. Not even
here long enough
to lament.

Today the breeze wears a fern:

Shiver
and living in the world, in
your brief green dress.

The amputated breast, like
a soul made out of flesh.

Masks

At the grocery store today —
these meteors and angels, wise men and all
the beautiful hallucinations of December, wearing
the masks of the Ordinary, the Annoyed, the Tired.
The Disturbed.
The Sane.

Only the recovering addict with his bucket and bell
has dared to come here without one.

He is Salvation.
His eyes have burned
holes in his radiance.
Instead of a mask, he has
unbuttoned his face.

The Accident

The Creator who dashed off a bird, who
snapped His fingers over the waters, and —
Holy shit. What is it?

A fish, He said. A lot
like a bird
except it swims.

*He's so
talented,* the other gods said of Him. But
that wasn't it. Like

the coffee of my subconscious spilled
all over my wedding dress, looking
down from such a distance:

What the poem must have looked like on the page
to the student assigned
to read it, who
could not read, and the way

it took me all semester
to understand what he was faking, because
the others, who
seemed to read, seemed
also not to understand.

Still, I should have guessed. Not
understanding made *them*
angry, while
He kept raising His hand to give me
better, stranger answers to my questions:

Consider daffodils.
Consider cancer.
Consider certain tiny lizards, and that

long before
anyone could count
there was still math.

The Invalid

The meadow this morning
from the window
of the waiting room.
Rainy, April, and impatient:

Meadowless.
Can't see a thing.

Can only hear
the kind of music children
make with instruments
constructed
of wood and string.

Simple. Damp
wind.
An invalid
long ago
who grabbed my wrist:

Where do you think you're going
in such a pretty little hurry, Miss?

THREE

from *Space, in Chains*

Where are the seats at the feast?

So we found ourselves in an ancient place, the very
air around us bound by chains. There was
stagnant water in which lightning
was reflected, like desperation
in a dying eye. Like science. Like
a dull rock plummeting through space, tossing
off flowers and veils, like a bride. And

also the subway.
Speed under ground.
And the way each body in the room appeared to be
a jar of wasps and flies that day — but, enchanted,
like frightened children's laughter.

Hospital parking lot, April

Once there was a woman who laughed for years uncontrollably
after a stroke.

Once there was a child who woke after surgery to find his parents
were impostors.

These seagulls above the parking lot today, made of hurricane and
ether, they

have flown directly out of the brain wearing little blue-gray masks,
like strangers' faces, full

of wingèd mania, like television in waiting rooms. Entertainment.
Pain. The rage

of fruit trees in April, and your car, which I parked in a shadow
before you died, decorated now with feathers,
and unrecognizable

with the windows unrolled
and the headlights on
and the engine still running
in the Parking Space of the Sun.

At the public pool

I could carry my father in my arms.
I was a small child.
He was a large, strong man.
Muscled, tan.
But he felt like a bearable memory in my arms.

The lion covers his tracks with his tail.
He goes to the terrible Euphrates and drinks.
He is snared there by a little shrub.
The hunter hears his cries, and hurries for his gun.

What of these public waters?

Come in, I said to my little son.
He stood at the edge, looking down.
It was a slowly rolling mirror.
A strange blue porcelain sheet.
A naked lake, transparent as a need.

The public life.
The Radio Songs.
Political Art.
The Hall of Stuff We Bought at the Mall. The plugged-up fountain at
        the center
of the Museum of Crap That Couldn't Last
has flooded it all.

Come in, I said again. *In here you can carry your mother in your arms.*

I can still see his beautiful belly forever.
The blond curls on his perfect head.
The whole Botticelli of it crawling on the surface
of the water. And
his sad, considerate expression.
No, he said.

Riddle

Most days I cling to a single word. It is a mild-mannered creature made of thought. *Future,* or *Past.* Never the other, obvious word. Whenever I reach out to touch that one, it scurries away.

Even my identity has been kept hidden from me. It is a child's ghost buried in mud. It is an old woman waving at me from a passing train. First, a multiplication. Then, a densification. Then, a pale thing draped carelessly over a bone.

Four weeks after my conception, I was given a tail. But then God had some mystical vision of all I might be — and took the tail back.

It required no violence, no surgery, no struggle, this quiet thievery, this snatching away of the deep, ancient secret. It would be true of everything:

My eyes closed, hands open, *Take it, take it.* Then, every day wasted chasing it.

The call of the one duck flying south

so far behind the others
in their neat little *v*, in their
competence of plans and wings, if
you didn't listen you would think
it was a cry for help
or sympathy —
friends! friends! —
but it isn't.

Silence of the turtle on its back in the street.
Silence of the polar bear pulling its wounded weight onto the ice.
Silence of the antelope with a broken leg.
Silence of the old dog asking for no further explanation.

How
was it I believed I was
God's favorite creature? I,
who carry my feathery skeleton across the sky now, calling
out for all of us. I, who am doubt now, with a song.

My beautiful soul

It is the beggar who thanks me profusely for the dollar.
It is a boat of such beggars sinking
beneath the weight of this one's thanking.

It is the bath growing cold around the crippled woman
calling to someone in another room.

And the arthritic children in the park
picking dust off summer
speck by speck
while a bored nurse watches.

The wind has toppled the telescope
over onto the lawn:
So much for stars.
Your brief shot at the universe, gone.

It is some water lilies and a skull in a decorative pond,
and a tiny goldfish swimming
like an animated change-purse
made of brightness and surprises
observing the moment through its empty eye.

Thank you, thank you, bless you, beautiful
lady with your beautiful soul…
It is as if I have tossed a postcard
of the ocean into the ocean.

My stupid dollar, my beautiful soul.

The photograph album in the junk shop

We are all the same, it claims. This
forgotten couple kissing
before the Christmas tree, in a year
they will be holding
the Christ child between them, whose
name they wish us to believe
is *Jim*.

Someone with a wheel.
A girl in a purple dress, squinting.
A wolf
rolling in ashes. A cake
bearing the Christ child's name. The waterfall
at the center of every life
spewing foam and beauty
onto the boats below. And also
the canyon into which will slip —

What is this on the rocks below?

The whole damn picnic?

And the shadow of that terrible
animal with horns
at every petting zoo. And
the Christ child in a costume
smoking cigarettes. The poisonous
brambles in bloom on a chain-link fence. A fat
man pretends to fly. A blond

woman laughs at a hand. The scoreboard. The lawn
mown. The family cat. (Here,
it is Acceptance. Here,
Malice.)

And beside them all, there is
Grandma

in a chair
staring at the future as she tells
a story without moving her lips. It is

a story to which the family
doesn't listen
because they are too busy
doing what families do.

And because it can't be true.

And still
her face waits on every page
like an ax left behind on the moon.

Memory of grief

I remember a four-legged animal strolling through a fire. Poverty in a prom dress. A girl in a bed trying to tune the AM radio to the voices of the dead. A temple constructed out of cobwebs into which the responsibilities of my daily life were swept. Driving through a Stop sign waving to the woman on the corner, who looked on, horrified.

But I remember, too, the way,
loving everyone equally because each of us would die,
I walked among the crowds of them, wearing
my disguise.
And how, when it was over, I found myself
here again
with a small plastic basket on my arm, just

another impatient immortal
sighing and fidgeting in an unmoving line.

Like a twentieth-century dream of Europe — all
horrors, and pastries — some part of me, for all time
stands in a short skirt in a hospital cafeteria line, with a tray, while

in another glittering tower named
for the world's richest man
my mother, who is dying, never dies.

(Bird
with one wing
in Purgatory, flying in circles.)

I wake up decades later, having dreamt I was crying.
My alarm clock seconds away
from its own alarm.

I wake up to its silence
every morning
at the same hour. The daughter
of the owner of the Laundromat
has washed my sheets in tears

and the soldiers marching across some flowery field in France
bear their own soft pottery in their arms — heart, lung, abdomen.

And the orderlies and the nurses and their clattering
carts roll on and on. In a tower. In a cloud. In a cafeteria line.

See, cold spy for time, who needs you now?

The knot

The knot in the mind. That pounding thought. The cricket all night. That bright singing knot. That meditation on knots, which is a goat. The child who will be the knot of its love. This love like a knot concealed in a cloud. This death-obsessed knot with a backache, a knot-ache, holding its eye to a microscope. This loosening knot, and its greatest hope. This knot that is energy transferred into form. The knot of an eye. Not asleep. Not awake. But waiting, this knot. Like machinery parked beneath a tent made of gauze. This cramped signature on a piece of paper. A thickening knot. An egg like a knot. Not a fist in a lake, this knot of a stranger. Not the bureaucrat's stamp on the folder of our fate. But a knot nonetheless, and not of our making.

The water glass. The rain. The scale
waiting for the weight. The car.
The key. The rag. The dust. Once

I was a much younger woman
in a hallway, and I saw you:

I said to myself
Here he comes.
My future's husband.

And even before that. I was the pink
throbbing of the swim bladder
inside a fish in the River Styx. I was
the needle's eye. I was the air
around the wing of a fly, and you

had no idea you were even alive.

My son practicing the violin

Some farmers with their creaking machinery moving slowly across a field. Some geese. The sun rising somewhere on some unripe peaches. I wander the labyrinth of that orchard. The foxes creep out of their dens to peek at me. Even my high heels are green.

Such love, and such music, it's a wonder Jesus doesn't make me spend every waking hour on my knees.

We've traveled here from a distant planet to teach you how to be a human being.

Even the paper cup in my hand has learned to breathe. And each note is a beautiful, ancient kingdom precariously balanced at the edge of a cliff above the sea.

View from glass door

I have stood here before.
Just this morning
I reached into the dark of the dishwasher
and stabbed my hand with a kitchen knife.

Bright splash of blood on the kitchen
floor. Astonishing
red. (All
that brightness inside me?)

My son, the Boy Scout, ran
to get the First Aid kit — while, beyond
the glass door, the orchard. Beyond

the orchard, the garden bed, and

beyond the garden, all
the simple people I remember
simply standing in their lines.
Or sitting in their chairs
waiting for the film to start
or for the plane to land
or for the physician to call them in.

How easy it would have been instead
to stand up shouting
about cold, dumb death.

But there they waited
as if the credits
might begin to roll again.
As if the bandages, the bolts, the scrolls. The paper
towels, the toilet paper. And

as the family stood around
considering my hand, I could clearly hear

the great silenced choirs of them
singing soothing songs:

Who fended for
and fed me. Who
lay beside me in the dark and
stroked my head. Who

called me their sweetheart, their
miracle child. Who
taught me to love
by loving me. Who, by dying, taught
me to die.

Covered in earth.
Covered in earth.
On the other side
of this glass door.
Calm, memorized
faces to the sky.

O elegant giant

These difficult matters of grace and scale:

The way music, our savior, is the marriage of math and antisocial behavior.

Like this woman with a bucket in the morning gathering gorgeous oxymora on the shore...

And my wildly troubled love for you, which labored gently in the garden all through June, then tore the flowers up with its fists in July.

Which set a place for you next to mine — the fork beside the spoon beside the knife (the linen napkin, and the centerpiece: a blue beheaded blossom floating in a bowl) — and even the red weight of my best efforts poured into your glass as a dark wine before I tossed the table onto its side.

Just another perfect night. Beyond destruction, and utterly unlikely, how some-one might have managed, blindly, to stumble on such a love in the middle of her life.

O elegant giant.

While, outside, the woods are silent.

And, overhead, not a single intelligent star in the sky.

The inner workings

This afternoon my son tore
his shorts climbing a barbed-wire fence. *Holy Toledo,* I said
when he crashed back through the cornstalks
with half of his shorts gone.

The sun was ringing its sonorous silent bell underground, as someone's
grandmother tucked
an awful little cactus under
a doily embroidered with buttercups.

In prisons

exhausted prisoners napped, having
brief and peaceful dreams, while beautiful girls in bikinis tossed
fitfully in their own shadows
on a beach

and somewhere else
in some man's secret garden shed
the watchmaker, the lens maker, the radio-

maker, the maker
of telescopes, of rhetorical devices:

The time-maker, the eye-maker, the voice-maker, the maker
of stars, of space, of comic surprises

bent together
over the future
clumsily tinkering with the inner
workings of its delights.

Look

Look! I bear into this room a platter piled high with the rage my mother felt toward my father! Yes, it's diamonds now. It's pearls, public humiliation, an angry dime-store clerk, a man passed out at the train station, a girl at the bookstore determined to read every fucking magazine on this shelf for free. They tell us that most of the billions of worlds beyond ours are simply desolate oceanless forfeits in space. But logic tells us there *must* be operas, there *have* to be car accidents cloaked in that fog. Down here, God just spat on a rock, and it became a geologist. God punched a hole in the drywall on Earth and pulled out of that darkness another god. She —

just kept her thoughts to herself. She just —

followed him around the house, and every time he turned a light on, she turned it off.

They say

one-twelfth of our lives is wasted
standing in a line.

The sacred path of that.

Ahead of me, a man in black, his broad back.
Behind me, a woman like me
unwinding her white veils.

And beyond us all, the ticket-taker, or the old
lady with our change, or

the officials with our food, our stamps, our unsigned papers, our
gas masks, our inoculations.

It hasn't happened yet.
It hasn't begun or ended.
It hasn't granted us its bliss
or exploded in our faces.
The baby watches the ceiling from its cradle.
The cat stares at the crack in the foundation.
The grandfather flies the sick child's kite higher
and higher. I set

my husband's silverware on the table.

I place a napkin beside my son's plate.

Soon enough,
but not tonight.
Ahead of us, that man's black back.
Behind us, her white veils.

Ahead of us, the nakedness, the gate.

Behind us, the serene errand-boy, the cigarette, the wink-
and-nod, the waiting.

Beyond that, too late.

We watch my father try to put on his shirt

Somewhere, my dead mother kneels at a trunk, her head and her arms all the way up as she tosses things over her shoulders, and cries.

The letters, the fading. The labyrinth, the cake. The four hundred brackish lakes of the brain. She searches for the
music, but she can't find it. Oh, God, it was here
only the other day.

He cannot do it. The shirt
slips to the floor. There is
dancing and laughter in hell, an angel weeping openly on a park bench in heaven.
My mother, dead and frantic in an attic. A white shirt on a floor. An old man in a wheelchair, rubbing his eyes. *Here it is, here it is!* the occupational therapists sing as they rise to the surface of the earth, smiling, bearing their terrible surprise.

Stolen shoes

for the woman who stole my shoes from the locker room at the gym

There is blood within the shoe
The shoe's too small for you

Such is the message in the cleft of the devil's foot
In the shrine piled high with sandals and pumps
In the shameless laughter of the younger women at Starbucks, leaning back,
    swinging their legs, full of foam, their cups

So much screaming in a small place
In a cage for a house cat, a cheetah

There is too much room in the shoe
The shoe's too big for you

The fish flopping in a bucket
Waddling through the orange grove, a wounded duck

So much screaming in that freedom
Butterfly on a windshield, clinging to a breeze

But, listen. I, too, stole something once only to stuff it in the trash

Together, me and you, thieves in one another's shoes at last

Or, better yet —
Have we *become* one another now, running barefoot in the grass

The mystical, final physics of that

Near misses

The truck that swerved to miss the stroller in which I slept.

My mother turning from the laundry basket just in time to see me open the third-story window to call to the cat.

In the car, on ice, something spinning and made of history snatched me back from the guardrail and set me down later between two gentle trees.

And that time I thought to look both ways on the one-way street.

And when the doorbell rang, and I didn't answer, and just before I slipped one night into a drunken dream, I remembered to blow out the candle burning on the table beside me.

It's a miracle, I tell you, this middle-aged woman scanning the cans on the grocery store shelf. Hidden in the works of a mysterious clock are her many deaths, and yet the whole world is piled up before her on a banquet table again today. The timer, broken. The sunset smeared across the horizon in the girlish cursive of the ocean, *Forever, For You.*

And still she can offer only her body as proof:

The way it moves a little slower every day. And the cells, ticking away. A crow pecking at a sweater. The last hour waiting patiently on a tray for her somewhere in the future. The spoon slipping quietly into the beautiful soup.

Cigarettes

Back then, we smoked them. In
every family photo, someone's smoking.

Such ashes, such sarcasm, the jokes
that once made loved ones
who are dead now laugh and laugh.

Cigarette in hand.
Standing glamorously at the mantel.
The fire glowing
ahead and behind
and all the little glasses
and the snow outside

filling up the birdbaths, the open graves, the eyes.

And the orchestras in gymnasiums!
That mismanagement
of sound. The wonderful
smoke afterward
in parking lots, in lungs. How

homeliness was always followed
by extravagance back then.
Like hearing lovemaking
in another room
or passing suffering
on the side of the road
without even slowing down:

So it is to remember
such times
and to see them again
so vividly in the mind.

Like a mysterious child
traveling toward us
on a moonless night
holding a jar
containing a light.

My son makes a gesture my mother used to make

My son makes a gesture my mother used to make. The sun in their eyes. Fluttering their fingers. As if to disperse it. The sun, like so many feverish bees.

I keep driving. One eye on the road, and one on the child in the rearview mirror. A man on the radio praying. The awful kid down the block where I was a child who buried a toad in a jar in the sandbox, dug it up a month later, and it was still alive.

He does it again. The sun, like the drifting ashes of a distant past. The petals of some exploded yellow roses.

The miracle of it.
The double helix of it.
The water running uphill of it.
Such pharmacy, in a world which failed her! She died before he was even alive, and here she is again, shining in his eyes.

Light nodding to light.
Time waving hello to time.
The ninety-nine names of Allah.
The sun extravagantly bright and full of radiant, preposterous spiritual advice — like a Bible rescued from a fire that killed a family of five:

I squint into it and see both a glorious parade of extinct and mythological beasts, and an illustration in a textbook of a protective sheath of protein wrapped around a strand of DNA — all cartoon spirals and billiard balls, and the sole hope of our biology teacher, Mr. Barcheski, who, finally enraged by the blank expressions on our faces, slammed it shut and walked away.

Riddle

We are a little something, God's riddle seems to suggest.

Little memories.
Little wisdoms.
Little matches,
bright or snuffed.

Where did my grandmother go when she pulled her curtains closed?

I watched her window fade
from the backseat of my father's car, thinking
She is ancientness. She has lived forever. It has driven her insane.

But the New Old.
When did they grow
So Old?

Some of them are sleeping in the hallway.
Some are in their rooms
listening to rock 'n' roll.

This moment of wisdom, I cast you off.

This grand foolishness, I embrace you.

And my father — the kindest, cleanest
man I'll ever know —
is spitting on the floor, demanding to know where I came from.

Briefly

Here and there some scrap of beauty gets snatched from this or that: One child's voice rising above the children's choir. A few wild notes of laughter passing through the open window of a passing car. That pink handkerchief waved at the parade. The tiny Nile-blue tile broken at the edge of the mosaic — all shining accident and awe. And this

last second or two of dreaming
in which your face
returns to me completely. Not
even needing to be, being

so alive again to me.

Space, in chains

Things that are beautiful, and die. Things that fall asleep in the afternoon, in sun. Things that laugh, then cover their mouths, ashamed of their teeth. A strong man pouring coffee into a cup. His hands shake, it spills. His wife falls to her knees when the telephone rings. *Hello? Goddammit, hello?*

Where is their child?

Hamster, tulips, love, gigantic squid. *To live.* I'm not endorsing it.

Any single, transcriptional event. The chromosomes of the roses. Flagella, cilia, all the filaments of touching, of feeling, of running your little hand hopelessly along the bricks.

Sky, stamped into flesh, bending over the sink to drink the *tour de force* of water.

It's all space, in chains — the chaos of birdsong after a rainstorm, the steam rising off the asphalt, a small boy in boots opening the back door, stepping out, and someone calling to him from the kitchen,

Sweetie, don't be gone too long.

Home

It would take forever to get there
but I would know it anywhere:

My white horse grazing in my blossomy field.
Its soft nostrils. The petals
falling from the trees into the stream.

The festival would be about to begin
in the dusky village in the distance. The doe
frozen at the edge of the grove:

She leaps. She vanishes. My face —
She has taken it. And my name —

(Although the plaintive lark in the tall
grass continues to say and to say it.)

Yes. This is the place.
Where my shining treasure has been waiting.
Where my shadow washes itself in my fountain.

A few graves among the roses. Some moss
on those. An ancient

bell in a steeple down the road
making no sound at all
as the monk pulls and pulls on the rope.

O elegant giant

And Jehovah. And Alzheimer. And a diamond of extraordinary size on the hand of a starving child. The quiet mob in a vacant lot. My father asleep in a chair in a warm corridor. While his boat, the Unsinkable, sits at the bottom of the ocean. While his boat, the Unsinkable, waits marooned on the shore. While his boat, the Unsinkable, sails on, and sails on.

FOUR

from *Lilies Without*

Where are the revels in the hall?

Prayer

Weren't we out of milk? And cheese? Did we not eat the cheese? The bread? Certainly that plastic bag was empty, maybe one stale piece. So how did it become this endlessness of bread? Whence came the dozen eggs, the whales and ravens, the herd of deer poured down the hillside, the bloody cardboard carton of eternal raspberries?

And why do such miracles and mysteries terrify me? Some secret file in some hive-like office complex — our name and address tucked away inside it. The beautiful suffering animals painted on the ancient walls of a cave. The ship's wake streaming from one shore to the other. Not just my family, the whole hungry country. *The species.* The children praying at an altar. The brakes of the truck screeching. The sun rising on a field of wheat. The sudden groceries. And, over it all, the spirit, like a snowy owl.

The eye of a sparrow, blinking.
The floating, and the falling.
The soundless waves of sad ecstatic memories.
Such freedom, such need.

At Gettysburg

The one I love stands at the edge
of a wheatfield wearing
a blue cap, holding
a plastic musket in his hands. The one I love does a goofy

dance at Devil's Den. Mans a cannon. Waves
at me from a hill. He

dips his foot into Bloody Run. The sepia
dream of his dead body
is pulled by the water
over the rocks. And I

am the shadow of a stranger taking
his picture, laid out like so much black
drapery on the pavement. Is there

some better explanation? Was there

some other mossy, meandering
path we might have taken

to this place through time and space? Why

is it that where my heart
should be, there's
a small bright horse instead? While I

was simply standing
over there by a stone, waiting, did
an old woman run her bony
hand through my hair
and leave this gray ribbon there?

The one I love leans up against a fence, and then
pretends to be shot. He

opens his eyes
wide and grabs his chest, stumbles
backward, falls
gracefully into the grass, where he lies

for a long time holding the sun in his arms. I take

another picture there. The worms
beneath him make

the burden of the earth seem light enough to bear — and still

inside me I believe I carry
the pond where the injured
swans have come to flock. I
believe I hold inside me
the lake into which the beautiful, armless
mortals wish to wade. I am

after all, their executioner and their creator, being
as I am, their mother. Were

they gods who came to Earth to die and suffer, I wonder, or

boys who died and turned to gods? Oh,

the one I love needs sunblock, I think, too late, and
perhaps a bottle of water, but now

I have no idea where we are. *Where*

were you, God asks, *when I*
spread out the heavens and the earth? If you

were not there, then

how can you expect to know where you are now? Truly

I don't know. I look around.
I say, *We're lost,*
to the one I love, who

looks over my shoulder and laughs. *No,*

Mom, he says
and points to dot and arrow
of ourselves on the map.

You're holding the battlefield upside down.

I Am the Coward Who Did Not Pick Up the Phone

I am the coward who did not pick up the phone, so as never to know. So many clocks and yardsticks dumped into an ocean.

I am the ox which drew the cart full of urgent messages straight into the river, emerging none the wiser on the opposite side, never looking back at all those floating envelopes and postcards, the wet ashes of some loved one's screams. How was I to know?   I am the warrior who killed the sparrow with a cannon. I am the guardian who led the child by the hand into the cloud, and emerged holding only an empty glove. Oh —

the digital ringing of it. The string of a kite of it, which I let go of. Oh, the commotion in the attic of it. In the front yard, in the backyard, in the driveway — all of which I heard nothing of, because I am the one who closed the windows and said, *This has nothing to do with us.*

In fact, I am the one singing this so loudly I cannot hear you even now. (Mama, what's happening outside? Honey, is that the phone?)

I am the one who sings:

The bones and shells of us.
The organic broth of us.
The Zen gong of us.
Oblivious, oblivious, oblivious.

Miss Post-Apocalypse

The shoes in the garden seemed
to know me by my name. Emptied, all of them, except

for the whispering of the breeze as it blew
over that emptiness and loosened
their tongues: *Girl,*
where

are all your trashy little daydreams now? (Oh,

my face on the page of a magazine
curled up in the fire. Me, smiling
on a big TV worshipping
a box of Tide.)

I couldn't bring myself to walk
home beneath that monstrous
cloud. I went

back to the factory instead.

I walked for miles.
But the gate was locked.
From somewhere inside,
I could hear

the last man on Earth
curse the last

card as he drew it from the deck.

The Thigh

Clothing and weapons set aside, I am simply your thigh, and proof
that underneath the world lies
a warm pool of water overflowing
with drowned blue butterflies.

All these years,
clear up to here:
As you waited, I waited too.
When you were tired,
I lay down with you.
You never noticed,
but now you do. (*That*
boy's fingers whispering past the hem of your skirt — guess who?)

Guess who.

Sleeve of moony, vaporous voices. The dead ebbing as the living flowed.
The calm milked cows in a field of clover. The long
white fish in a bath. Cellular
shadow on the forest floor. Someone withdraws
a shining sword.
The naked man standing on the deck with his harpoon.
So much water lapping at a mindless shore. So
much spring stuffed into a pale
silk sack.
Or a club

tossed down among the flowers.

I am your memory
of it all, your life, in flesh and hours, statement,
and tone, meat, and weather

wrapped around a bone.

Elegy

And now, it's all the same
to you —

the mouth, the sink, the dream.

A bed at the edge of an ocean's the same
as a train speeding
through Germany.

The Bureau of Travels
has approved all your plans, so you
no longer need

your passport, your cell phone, your coat

to blaze screaming
through the vast North, waving

a flag on fire in the snowy forest, pouring

wine all over the ground, draping
the rearview mirrors
of my car
with red cloth, fogging

the windows, locking the doors, staging

all this silence and emptiness and rust
to torment me, to reveal to me
the hidden mechanics
of lust, having

graduated,
as you did this morning, from being
just another humble student of the universe

to its greatest authority.

Miss Estrogen

To have been a storm in a suit of armor. (Or the hound

tied up outside
as the fox slipped quivering through the field.) To have been

fever in an envelope
mailed to a fire (while

a man in the bedroom shouted, having

mortally wounded himself
while sharpening his own knife). Like

unpredictable furniture
for many years. (*She
has her period, she's madly in love, leave
her alone, she's out of her mind*). Or like

a red carpet rolled through a forest, ending at an ocean.
(What

will become of your life
without such desire?) To have been

the wind in the kitchen, which blew
the plates and bowls from the cupboards, as the oven

door lolled open. Or a dormouse
in a wineglass. Such
sacred fury. (Was it meaningless?) Pageant

in a matchbox. All
the mirrors and tiaras locked up in a vault, as I

scaled, in my satin robe, the prison walls, ran
straight into the burning church in my burning stilettos.
(And then

so many bewildered, dusty knickknacks on a shelf.

For Sale: *Curios.*
Everything must go.)

Once, someone
nodded in my direction as I did my job. "She's

the temporary girl here" — meaning me. Once

someone pointed and said, "Look
at that wild bird in that tree."

I looked
too late. It had flown away.
To have been

that bird, and to become that tree.

My Father's Closet

The birdlessness of a winter night is in it. The phantom lover writing letters on the wind.

Well, Laura, you always wanted a sailboat, didn't you? You wanted an aeolian harp. You wanted a white room filled with white flowers. Well, here it is. Here we sit, waiting for a woman wounded with light to call us in. This is your father's name on her lips. This is the village into which we've slipped. In the night. Via pills. With cataracts, aneurysms, fractured hips. That little apprehension? Yes. This was it. The subliminal message in the mist at the edges of the screen? All those years, all that peace, you could barely repress this scream.

Listen: A chorus a million miles away is singing *Solace, solaced, don't be ridiculous.*

The only suit my father ever owned is in it. The psyche's anchor sunk deep in an ocean of thoughtlessness. A child brooding over her own origins, making crystals in a dish — in it. All the plans of animals — their blueprints and files, the envelopes on which they scrawled their desperate grocery lists:

A silence follows it.
A silence preceded it.
This was it.
This is it.

Kindergarten. There was

a cherry tree planted outside the classroom, a little brass plaque

in dirt. In
May, it shrieked into blossom, and I thought *"We've*

planted this tree in his memory" meant

that although this child who'd come before us
had already been dead for years, there

was still somehow a final tree
they'd managed to place
forever in his head.

In May, it burst into pastel
flames, or the tips of the fingers of a resurrected child: *1947–1953,*
We've

planted this tree
in his memory.

Oh, what would it be like, I wondered then,

to have that thing explode
each year for a week into blossom in your head

so long after you were dead?

And now,
each May, when I
close my eyes, and see
all of them again

file out of darkness

in their black clothes

into sun poured all over a parking lot radiant with chrome, like

a branch of involuntary, perennial, screaming
light in my memory, I know.

Stroke

The shadow
of the migration
on the ground

and a subtle girl with a rope.

This is the Styx, and the floodlight on the ferry, and the expressionless man with his pet jackal. The mattress strapped to your back. The bees and the scenery in your pot roast, mashed. The delicious shame of that. And the concentration. And desire. And your soul on a flagpole on the other side.

Where? Where?

It doesn't matter. They will take you only halfway there.

The Bad Teacher

She could come to the door in September for our son.

All thistled cursive and miscounted nickels. She
might tell him facts he'll recall all his life:

Mice are spontaneously
generated by garbage.
The size of the skull is the size of the mind.
At the end of all this love
and fuss, we die. *Everything*
your mother told you about eternity was a lie.

I imagine her at night at a desk made for a child.
Her knees too high. Her elbows
rest on the floor. Switched

off for summer. An awful
doll. (*I should have burned her as a girl, this has gone too far.*)
Her spine and her eyes have been
sewn closed
by the same seamstress
who sewed this:

a black felt scrap of nightmare, its
edges stitched up sloppily to the stars.

Miss Consolation for Emotional Damages

When the embarrassment began, no one could see it. It lived

in the closet, the basement, the attic, the brain. It was
a moth at first, and then it was the hole a moth had made.

It had to do with unemployment: No! (Who
cared that my father couldn't work?) It had

to do with the boy next door, who'd
seen my mother drunk, whose
own mother had explained to him
that it wasn't our fault we were poor.

No.

It had been born
in another country. It had come to this one on a boat.
It couldn't speak the language. It had
left a wolf
on the other shore. (A tame
wolf: someone
had beaten the wildness out of it
with kindness, and a stick.) It had

to do with paradox, that space was transparent
and also dense.
It had to do with Einstein.
The curvature of the world in a third dimension. It couldn't
take the contradiction, woke
one morning as a careless
American girl, mouth
stuffed with pink
fluff: When

she opened it, for centuries, nothing
but pleasant inanities came out.

Fashion Victim

Too much mist to see the mountain. The freeway
lost in fog. The garden — a mirage. I order clothes
all day from catalogues (a bird

flies into a cloud
and never flies back out) like

a passenger on a doomed flight, raising
her glass in a toast
to the pilot, to the sky. They arrive

in long white boxes and in whispers
on the porch, like winter. Soon

there will be nothing but obscurity
as far as the eye can see. Until

there's only one leaf left

clinging to one tree. Until, like

my father over there in his chair, my
clothes are how you know it's me.

Poem Ending in Lines from Jarrell

This morning, a dead mouse
under the kitchen counter. It had

a postcard of the cosmos in its eye. I was trying,

simply, to take the garbage out, but

shrieked when I saw it and slammed the cupboard shut.

By noon, the light
in the living room
is irrationally bright. The candy dish is full
of small, hard pleasures. I live

in a quiet suburb. The jets

make childish sounds
in the sky. My

book on the couch is a bird in a pond
pushing itself somewhere with one bent wing… but I've

seen snapshots of my own child, wide-eyed, with his

whole life before him, a pinprick

of light in his eye
like an exquisite diamond viewed
from a dizzying height.

And I've been blinded by it:

If only you knew there would be something else, that
a thimbleful of what
you'd been

would continue to exist.

If only you could rise
from death
as you once rose from sleep, as a child,

and walk through the rooms at night, fingering
the things
in the deep blue light, thinking, *Who*

was my mother before she was my mother, my

father, the clock? Ticking. The television, off.
But

this is imagination's light. Outside,

the trees, anesthetized. And the stars
mass silently in the sky. *They*

said, "Here are the maps";
we burned the cities. The people

are punishing the people — why?

Miss Congeniality

There's a name given
after your death
and a name you must answer to while you're alive.

Like flowers, my friends — nodding, nodding. My
enemies, like space, drifting
away. They

praised my face, my enunciation, the power
I freely relinquished, and the fires

burning in the basements of my churches,
and the pendulums swinging
above my towers.
And my

heart (which was a Boy Scout

lost for years in a forest). And my

soul (although the judges said
it weighed almost nothing
for goodness had devoured it).

They praised my feet, the shoes
on my feet, my feet
on the floor, the floor —
and then

the sense of despair
I evoked with my smile, the song

I sang. The speech
I gave

about peace, in praise of the war. Oh,

they could not grant me the title I wanted

so they gave me the title I bore,

and stubbornly refused
to believe I was dead
long after my bloody mattress
had washed up on the shore.

War with Toy Soldiers

They have fallen off the coffee table
onto the floor. They have slipped
under rugs, lost
their guns, found

themselves in the strange
gray dream between
the floral cushions and the upholstery. They

have been batted all over the house by the cat, dropped
their canteens
down the register grates, forgotten

their homelands, their languages, their names. They

have fallen out of love.
Boarded the wrong trains.
Laughed loud and long late into the night
while digging their own graves. They

have bathed in rain. Trudged through mud. Been
drunk. Driven

in long convoys of trucks without brakes across desert plains.

They have stood at the edges
of swiftly moving rivers, watching

time flounder down to the ocean, singing,
Once, there was not even a plan.
A plan still had to be made.

Now, it's Monday. September.
The children have vanished
from the dream of their summer vacation, and

a mother, on her knees, alone
in the house for the first time in months
could assess this situation, could see

how the pure white deer that always wanders

onto the battlefield
after the violence

stands now at the center
of the wonder in silence.

Miss Weariness

At first she looked like all the other girls, but then

the chipped fingernail, and then

she sat down in a folding chair
and let the other girls pass by

in their ball gowns, in their bathing suits, in their
beatific smiles, but she

had tossed her heels aside.

Enough of industry, enough
of goals and troubles, looking ahead, grooming, and dreaming
and anything that ended
in *i-n-g* in this
life ever again, she said.

Oh, enough, even, of the simple stuff:

The will-o'-the-wisp, the rain on a lake, all
those goldfish in their plastic
baggies at the fair. To them

it must have been
as if the world were divided
into small warped dreams, nowhere

to get to, and nothing to do but swim.

New Dress

Dress of dreams and portents, worn

in memory, despite
the posted warnings
sunk deeply into the damp
sand
all along the shore. (*The green*

tragedy of the sea
about to happen to me.) Even

in my subconscious, I ignored them.
(*The green*

eternity of the sea, just around the corner.) That

whole ominous summer, I wore it, just
an intimation
then, a bit
of threatening ephemera. Another
rumor. Another
vicious whisper. And then
they sang. (*The giddy*

green
girls
of the sea.)

The feminine

maelstrom
of it, I wore. (*How*

quiet, at the edge of it, the riot. How

tiny, the police.) The *Sturm*

und Drang of it. The crypt
and mystery. The knife
in fog of it. The haunted
city of my enemy.
(*And always*
the green, floating, open
book of the sea.) That

dress, like

an era of deafness and imminent error, ending
even as I wore it, even as I dragged the damp

hem of it
everywhere
I wore it.

I made the gown myself from minutes
held together with safety pins, and

wore it as I wafted through the nursery,
pouring light all over the crowns
of their heads. All

those ghostly babies in their rows. *Oh,*

you swear you'll remember us forever,
but you won't.

FIVE

from *Gardening in the Dark*

Alas for the bright cup!

Alcoholism

It had nothing to do with how much they drank:

How much they drank!
The Christmas tree lit like a ladder on fire.
The heart like a kerosene lamp.

In France, a little dog
who could dance the minuet.
In Vienna, a deaf man writing symphonies in an attic.

Strange things happened in our house
the hour after happy hour. Call

that one the Hour
of the Tender Parent, Hour of the Big Happy Plan.
Love and tears and bravado, and a patience
like dust settling on a slab

of marble
in a cathedral
in a small medieval town, a town

in which our ancestors
laughed, passing a flask.

That was the flask in which I was conceived.
The test tube the world was made in.

A blue vapor rose
swirling from its throat, a thin
veil that became the cosmos.

And, somewhere, a linear accelerator, waiting.
An atomic number assigned
to every one of us.

This homeland, a prologue.
This country with no king

except its mercurial soul. Its spirit. Its tincture.
Somewhere… stars, sex, libraries, and that
music I'd been waiting
all my life to hear. Where
was Bach before he reached my ears?

Bach, in the half-finished basement.
Beethoven in the snow at the television's borders.

A beggar somewhere found
a ten-dollar bill in the street.
Oh, Bach

was everywhere I didn't listen.
At the bottom of the fountain at the center of the mall —
all those shiny coins, I could
have dipped my hands right in
if I hadn't been afraid to get caught.

And the forests, full of evergreen!
Moss and pine and the canned scent of spring.

They were perfectly happy
for a long, long time. When I
close my eyes I can see them still
wearing the fabric my memory is made of —

inexpensive, easy to clean.
They were everything to me

in their plaid clothes
on our plaid couch.

What do you think?

BOOK TITLE: _____

COMMENTS: _____

_____

_____

_____

OUR MISSION:

Poetry is vital to language and living. Copper Canyon Press publishes extraordinary poetry from around the world to engage the imaginations and intellects of readers.

Can we quote you? ☐ yes ☐ no

☐ Please send me a catalog full of poems and email news on forthcoming titles, readings, and poetry events.

☐ Please send me information on becoming a patron of Copper Canyon Press.

NAME: _____

ADDRESS: _____

CITY: _____ STATE: _____ ZIP: _____

EMAIL: _____

Thank you for your thoughts!

MAIL THIS CARD, SHARE YOUR COMMENTS ON FACEBOOK OR TWITTER, OR EMAIL POETRY@COPPERCANYONPRESS.ORG

Copper Canyon Press

A nonprofit publisher dedicated to poetry

CopperCanyonPress.org

BUSINESS REPLY MAIL
FIRST-CLASS MAIL   PERMIT NO. 43   PORT TOWNSEND WA

POSTAGE WILL BE PAID BY ADDRESSEE

Copper Canyon Press
PO Box 271
Port Townsend, WA 98368-9931

The Internet

The first time I sit down to it alone
I am flesh surrounded by space.

The space begins at the edges of my body
and from there it expands to contain

everything.

I've sinned.
Cannot be saved.
Surrounding me is this strange haze
made of information.

There are owls trapped in barns
on fire. Hysterical, with wings.
There are statues dumped
into the sea, the sea is full of these.

There are things I've said and done that still belong to me.
And the silence

in which they're packaged
accumulates like time, while through the window I see
a crane skid to a halt on the pond:
He was a child. Surely
he went to heaven.
It's been years since that boy died. What
makes me think I could talk to him now?

Black Dress

I could go no further than that first line:
Spring comes even to the closet.
The words like little iron blossoms on a vine.

The parks full of people under a heathery sky.
The music of silverware, of violins.
Near the road, a woman paints
the pickets of her fence with blinding light.

When Herod sat down at the table, the roasted
bird flew from the platter crying, "Christ lives! He is alive!"
It's spring, even at night.
The mushrooms damply reflect the stars.
All manner of pale flesh, opened up like eyes. Moonlight

on the jellyfish. In the dark
grass, the startling muteness of a child's
white rubber rat.

But the closet. Even

in spring, the closet's a blind hive. A black dress —

hangs at its center — like Persephone, it's

the closet's prisoner
and its queen. *Never forget,*
it sings. *I saw you then. I saw it all:*

After the funeral, the riotous dance. After the wedding, the long

weeping and kneeling in the bathroom stall.

Oh, there are birds the world's
entirely forgotten (winter, amnesia) singing again
to the comings and the goings, the bright

and empty flashes,
the openings and closings. *Sweetheart,
I'm leaving. Honey, I'm home.* But that

black dress hangs always and omniscient in its single thought, its

accumulating mass — a darkness
tucked into another darkness:
where I wore it first,

where I'll wear it last.

"Today, a Thief Who Stole Beehives, Hanged"

excerpt from *A Hangman's Diary:* October 12, 15 —

My son with his arms raised above him
in a wheatfield
in October

is a bit of folk art.

His eyes are made from bottle caps.
Straw, his hair, and rubber bands.

But I have left the shadow
of my hand upon his making.
A scrap of breath and ghost.
A cold, slow planet passes over.

In Nuremberg, Dürer
sketches a study for Christ's robe, or
two beautiful hands, folded — while

on the bridge outside his window

the hangman waits with his rope.

Speeding Ticket

The officer asks if I know
why it is I've been pulled over. Oh,
no, I say, not

that armed robbery back in '88? It is a joke

only a woman with two
children in the car, a woman
of a certain age could make. There's a small

pleasant birthmark shaped
like an island I've been to on his face.
I show him the proper papers. Yes,

I've been to that place,
and I know about narrow escapes — so

many sputtering coals
tossed into the mossy shadows among
the forget-me-nots, the violets, the wild oregano.

In a hurry, ma'am, today?

Hell no.
We could have been early
or late. Who cared? They never unlock that gate. What
difference would it make?
What I was after was just
a graceful passage to another place,
and now I know there's no such thing.

A flock of swans
risen from the lake.

No swans. No way.
The self, contrary
to popular opinion, is *not*

the thing that remains. We are
infinite, and it isn't
a question, is it,
of whether or not we could be replaced. Who

among the millions of us
would be worth the trouble it would take?

Truly, I wanted only
to *appear* to obtain such grace, and then

through the years somehow I became
a high brick wall fully expecting
the little blue flowers to thrive in my shade.

Once, I let a crescent wrench
rust for years in snow and rain. I knew

exactly where I'd dropped it, could
have taken you to the high
grass into which I'd let it slip, but there it stayed

until I saw the paperboy pick it up
and put it in his pocket one day.
Strange, only
the other morning
my son said he wanted
to be a policeman, or a demon, when he grew up.
To get bad people, he said.

And I said yes, and I poured more
coffee into my cup, and I

remembered the signs, that the signs
were posted all over that place:

Thin Ice, No Skating.

We skated anyway.

The yellow tape.
The psychology majors.
The structuralists, the policymakers. And how,
when the time finally came
to stand before them and try to explain,

I had nothing at all to say.

Only to find myself suddenly unable
any longer not to say it, finally

having you
here like this, all
ears and leaning
into my window with an island on your face.

True enough, I was not yet naked.
Comprehensive collision, the neighborhood was safe.

I had an address in it, and a name. Only

to find you
this patient beside
my motor vehicle in your final disguise, all
merciless kindness, laughing a little, with a boy's
turquoise eyes.

A voice says, *Hurry, I'm burning.*
A voice says, *Where are you hurt?*

All those years, I thought
if only there were a fine, I could pay it
wholly, and this slow torture would be over!

A voice says, *This*
isn't the end,
you know, no
monologue can save you.
A voice says, *Yes, Officer, I know*

why it is I've been pulled over,

while you write it down,
as I always knew you would.
This gentle reckoning,
all my life

I was driving toward it as fast as I could.

The Second Week of May

What will we buy with Judas's money?
Who will live in Hitler's house? What

shall we do with this veil stolen

from the murdered bride, this
blanket lifted from the sleeping child?

I will buy candy, says the sweetheart.
I will grow here, the primrose sings.

The lightness of silk in a perfumed breeze —
soft as cashmere, pale pink.

Where can we build
the house of spring,

the one built
on a clear conscience, the one
in which no innocent

civilian has ever been killed?
Yes. Imagine.
Every day
a clean kitchen, every night, a Puritan's pillow.

But it's May, and the lilac
whispers to the wisteria,
*Whose shadow shall I wear
this year to the prom? Whose*

*white scarf sewn from a virgin's
last breath is this?*

Macaroni & Cheese

One day you may be asked, "How
was it that God brought forth
Being

out of Nothing?" Then, "Is
there no difference between them,
Nothing — and Being?" Outside

a strange slow snow, and a big
black bird hunched
over something in the road. The sky

will be a pale

reflection of itself,
like a woman making dreamy circles
at the center of a dish with a cloth.

Love. Hunger. Other alchemies.
You may be asked, "What

are my eyes made of? Can
Santa's reindeer be burned by fire? In
heaven, does Jesus eat?"
In the oven, something breathing.
Rising. Melting. Shifting
shape and sweetening
in the heat. Now

you can see this bird in the street
is wrestling something bloody

out of a carcass, trying
to expose its heart. You

put the dish down beside the cloth, and say,
"Darling, I don't know."

There's a small one in my brain

beyond the tiny house, the lawn
mowed by the miniature mower, the mall
and its matchbox cars parked in the little lot.

There's also an ocean
no bigger than the opal
my mother once wore on her left hand. At night

the fish still nibble
the flesh of her fingers in it. And a casino

the size of a sequin.
A cathedral, like a seed.

But it's the forest that waits for me.

How many times in this life
have I wished to be alone?

The other children were throwing

sand on the beach. The elderly
aunt, who wanted
me to sit on her lap. Someone

humming in the library, whistling
in the elevator. The check-
out line, the sidewalk sale, the tourists

leaning over the railing
to get a better look at the falls, climbing

the stairs behind me
to the top of the Eiffel Tower.

Midnight, the baby cries.

The phone: The same
friend with her
same broken heart in Saskatchewan.

The Greyhound bus. The party. The kiss. The man
in the waiting room who wanted
to tell me about his cyst.

In that forest, I will.

Classroom strangely empty. Children grown.
No one's come to see
this particular movie but me. Not

another pair of headlights
on the highway, not
only for miles, for good.

It's a small forest, but the only path through it

ends where it began. It waits

at the edge of the rest of it for me

saving up names and faces
I won't be needing again.

World Peace

A day like a mayfly on which someone slammed a Bible, all

exoskeletal radiance and insignificance in the dark. We find

ourselves the only
mother and child
who decided it was wise in this storm-impending crisis

to come to the county fair.

Sheep among strangers. One
lone pony tethered to a pole. The prize
pig speaks eloquently in his sleep
on the tired subject of world peace, and the devil, who

owns all this fairness outright, sits
in a chair over there
by the fence
and lets his dog sniff around at the air. Briefly

it's air
made from the kind of paper
the repo men roll through the halls of the house
to keep the mud on their boots from ruining your rugs
on the day that they stomp
in and out
with all the things you ever bought on credit,
which, in the end, was everything you had:

As Grandma used to say,
We're going to have some weather.

But, at the moment, like petals —
a soft spray of spit, we are made of it.
And love, that slut, just

runs around deep-kissing everyone. So why

are we blind
to her wild suppositions
99 percent of the time?

Or does love generally never love us quite this much?

Well, might it suffice to say today I am struck dumb
by the laughable notion of numbers,

the whole hilarious idea of *greed*?
And the absurdity of feeling anything but peace
flies right over my head
like a flock of alarm clocks in the breeze.

Yes, Grandma, *God rest your soul*, we
will definitely have some weather,

but, for now,
the rides are quiet, the fun house is free, there are
no lines,

and at every gate a patient man or woman waits
for our tickets
with an open hand and a smile.

Inscriptions on Wax Tablets

Spring break, I'm sixteen. A drunk
girl on a balcony in a sundress
with a piña colada.
Burning, I'm about

to slip out of my own memory altogether —

still dancing, however, still
talking nonsense to a stranger in a salmon-
pink suit according to my friends.

Memory, like a shoebox full of ocean.
This life like the forgotten plot of a novel:

Oh, the protagonist wakes up early. She grows older.

But, through it all, this body, also, full of blood and thought.
This body, a heavy bubble.

And, under me, a little net
my mother sewed for me
out of naïveté
and luck.

Sacred Flower Watching Me

Deep in the ground, in the center
of a bulb, in the scarlet
darkness wrapped in crackling

there is a pinprick
of light. It's hot. It stirs. It's spring —
pitiful and sweet as a small girl spanked.

My love, all of it, a life of it, has been
too little. Nor has my rage ever forced any diamonds
out of the blood through the skin.

How awful
resurrection
for someone like me will be. The teenage
girls being dragged

out of the earth by their hair.

Tongues, testicles, plums, and small hearts bloat
sweetly in the trees. And then

a silence like water
poured into honey —

the silence of middle age.

But there are nights I feel a sacred
flower watching me.
Such affection!
Even in my cradle, it was waiting
warmly, its soft

white gaze

steady on my insufficient face.

Hardware Store in a Town without Men

I found myself in a story
without suspense, only
one deaf falcon circling deafly, and that
wild college girl next door

screaming at her mother on the phone.

My heart, a golden lobster, a star
in a grave, some
hot blood running underground...

and all my early daydreams loosed
like termites in the walls
of some deserted church.

Oh, I recognized my agony right away.
The howling dog of daylight life. The years
of lust had opened up
a permanent inn for phantoms in my brain.

Then, I turned forty.
Every morning

sweeping out the shadows
from the cobwebbed corners, raking
the leaves from the gutters,
the hair from the drains...

And sleep, the sweet
rolling water of its *e*'s.
A stroll through the beautiful
ruins of my own dreams.
A hardware store
in a town without men. Whole

shelves devoted to wrenches, gleaming,

and no reason
to lock the door.

No door.

Eighteen Days of Rain

July/August 2000

The rain in the gutter sings the kind of song
women sing when they're falling out of love.

Or the kind of song I sang to my mother
her last night on the oncology ward.

Rain, certainly, but *eighteen days?*

Death, of course, but why this way?

At the end of it, the Bible says, God
sends a pastel cliché,
a brilliant bit of kitsch:
Something to piss off the cynics, or for
little girls to decorate their bedrooms with, this

symbol for cheerfulness, a pot of gold at the end of it.

But do You remember how she wept?

For half an hour they had
to tap the back of her hand
until one last vein that hadn't
already been wrecked could be had.
And then

those long last days. A creature
with wings kept pulling her under
then dragging her back to the surface again.
God? Remember,

when she wasn't drowning in her own lungs
we played a game of cards. Hey, is that

You up there behind those weighty clouds?
Do You hold a sparrow gently in Your hand,
plucking the feathers from it
one by one?

God, forgive me, I didn't mean for this
to turn into
another protest song:

There have been other bodies,
other waters.
Please don't think
that I've forgotten.
Once, I lay

at the edge of one
with my hair spread out on the sand
while the sea tried to enter me.

Behind me, on a blanket, a naked boy played
"Blowin' in the Wind" on his guitar.

Then, I was young. I thought
that I was God. I thought

silence was a prayer.
And some nights, certainly, listening
to my own heartbeat in the dark, what

I still hear is his blond dog
chasing a stick into the warm waves there.

Inscriptions on Wax Tablets

Later, the football coach's son
will carry me to bed
and leave me there, untouched. I'll

wake up with one arm flung into my suitcase, the other
covering my face.

I had been wandering in a staticky meadow
for a long time, gathering
intangible flowers and humming
a single note — or so it seemed to me

until someone showed me a photo:

There I was, indisputably, in the corner, neither

myself nor anyone else. Sixteen, spring
break, sipping a piña colada, and tottering

at the edge of a balcony
in high heels while, below me,
that airy net
blew around in the breeze.

I'd never be able to recall a thing, but my
friends would swear I danced all night
with the same guy (pink

suit, my arms around his neck)
and that, after he left, I

lay laughing for a long time
on the damp lawn, while
the world —

made of danger, made of weight—
spun on without me
and despite me
for someone else's sake.

Happy Meal

for Jack

At the bottom of the bag, there is a fact
(a bit of joy, a bit of junk) which my son was issued

from the womb into this world knowing.

All those years, the way we lived!
So much gardening in the dark.
Or an old blind woman sewing
a tremulous rose on a tablecloth. *Have*

a great night, the boy
at the second drive-thru window says. He smiles

like a boy who woke
only moments ago
to the sound of a moth
in a city made of linen.

Autumn already, and the showy
flowers are over, retreated
into the earth. It simply

means what it is:
Neither beginning
nor fin de siècle

regardless of the way it feels. Unlike

the child in the car seat behind me, I'm
old enough to remember
when the television used to sign off.
"The Star-Spangled Banner"

and a flag in the wind
followed by nothing but fuzz. How

many nights
I woke to that fuzz, a girl
in the center of a dress
made of electrical dust.

For years, I watched the news, and still
I saw this world
as through a shower door, steamily, and taught
my child to speak
of the griefs of the past
in silly words and song:

Boo-boo, ashes, we all fall down.

But, once, a father bolted the doors
and said to his family, *We*
must allow our friends and neighbors
to call on us no more.

It is a little monster, this fact
at the bottom of the bag, this complimentary toy.
And to the child behind me, it seems
completely free, despite the price.

O Happy Meal: even happier, the *happiest*
meal of our lives! No

end of the world. No horizon on fire.
And a blessing before I forget:

May some beautiful evening in the future find you

sipping wine with your beloved
in a peaceful foreign country

while the lake moves full of shredded moon
and tiny candlelit fish

and the sound of a violin
played expertly in another room

and my death, if it has come, not troubling you a bit.

SIX

from *Dance and Disappear*

Alas for the mailed warrior!

Clown

It was summer, and the clown had come
to the same restaurant to which we'd come
for a piece of strawberry pie.
Big white smile.
Wig of fire.

The sun had begun to set
with a piece of gold in its mouth.
There were devils in the Dumpsters eating flies.
What's that? the three-year-old asked.
I said, *She is a clown.*

Time had begun to pass so fast I felt
as if the weekly newspaper came to our house every day, yet
I had a photograph of myself
in which I'd blown my bangs back, wanting
to have wings like an angel, or Farrah Fawcett

when what I had was hair
that made me look in this photograph
like a girl who'd lived for a while
in another century, on a distant planet.
Someday my children would laugh.

She's not a woman, the three-year-old said
of the clown. There were
white seeds blowing around in the evening breeze
without a plan, landing their fluff-craft in
the Big Boy parking lot, onto the hoods of cars.

*A man puts a gun to your head and demands
your child, what should you do?* That's
the kind of early summer night it was.
The kind of night in which, perhaps,
you have a last moment

to look around and laugh — at
the child, and the clown, and the pie, and the fact
that if each atom could be collapsed
into a sphere no bigger than its core, all
of the Washington Monument could be crammed

into a space no bigger than an eraser.
How modest were your desires!
In the order of things, it's true
a clown is last, but all of us are futile
when it comes to want

and stupid to look at in a restaurant.

Stay in this world with me.

There go the ships.
The little buses.
The sanctity, the subway.
But let us stay.

Every world has pain.
I knew it when I brought you

to this one. It's true —
the rain is never stopped
by the children's parade. Still

I tell you, it weakens
you after a while into love.

The plastic cow, the plastic barn.
The fat yellow pencil, the smell of paste.

Oh, I knew it wasn't perfect
all along.
Its tears and gravities.
Its spaces and caves.
As I know it again today

crossing the street
your hand in mine
heads bowed in a driving rain.

Buffalo

I had the baby in my arms, he was asleep.
We were waiting for Old Faithful, who was late.
The tourists smelled like flowers, or

like shafts of perfume moving
from bench to bench, from
gift shop to port-o-pot. The sun

was a fluid smear in the sky, like
white hair in water. The women
were as beautiful as the men, who

were so beautiful they never needed
to see their wives or children again.

It happened then.

Something underground. The hush of sound.

I remembered
once pretending
to have eaten a butterfly.
My mother held my arms hard until
I told her it was a lie

and then she sighed. I've

loved every minute of my life!
The day I learned to ride a bike
without training wheels, I

might as well have been riding a bike
with no wheels at all! If

at any time I'd

had to agree to bear
twenty-seven sorrows
for a single one of these joys…

If the agreement were that I
had to love it all so much
just, in the end, to die…

Still, I can taste those wings I didn't eat, the sweet
and tender lavender of them. One

tourist covered her mouth
with a hand
and seemed to cry. How

could I have doubted her?
There were real tears in her eyes! The daisies

fell from her dress, and if
at that moment
she'd cracked an egg in a bowl,

the bowl would have filled with light. If

there is a God, why not

this violent froth, this
huge chiffon scarf
of pressure under water under her
white sandals in July?

The baby was asleep, still sucking, in my arms, a lazy

wand of sun moved
back and forth across his brow. I heard a girl's laughter

in the parking lot, soft
and wild as

the last note of "Jacob's Ladder"
played by the children's handbell choir.

I turned around.

It had been watching me. Or him. Or both of us.

Good beast, I whispered to it
facetiously under my breath.
It took, in our direction, one

slow and shaggy step.

Spontaneous Human Combustion:
An Introduction

She was waiting for her husband in the kitchen (cup
of coffee, slice of chiffon pie) when he came in tossing
beneath his burning hair. A thing like this can happen

to anyone, anywhere

but especially in the West, full
as it is
of dreaming and fading, and

especially in the U.S.
where we have become child-
like strangers in the place we've made.

The basement
full of batteries and cables. Outside, the
magnolia full of snow.
It was winter, they were older, all

her little phobias —

sinusitis, pneumonia —

when her husband stepped into the kitchen
thrashing around in his new clothes.

Bike Ride with Older Boys

The one I didn't go on.

I was thirteen,
and they were older.
I'd met them at the public pool. I must

have given them my number. I'm sure

I'd given them my number,
knowing the girl I was…

It was summer. My afternoons
were made of time and vinyl.
My mother worked,
but I had a bike. They wanted

to go for a ride.
Just me and them. I said
okay fine, I'd
meet them at the Stop-N-Go
at four o'clock.
And then I didn't show.

I have been given a little gift —
something sweet
and inexpensive, something
I never worked or asked or said
thank you for, most
days not aware
of what I have been given, or what I missed —

because it's that, too, isn't it?
I never saw those boys again.

I'm not as dumb
as they think I am

but neither am I wise. Perhaps

it is the best
afternoon of my life. Two
cute and older boys
pedaling beside me — respectful, awed. When we

turn down my street, the other girls see me...

Everything as I imagined it would be.

Or, I am in a vacant field. When I
stand up again, there are bits of glass and gravel
ground into my knees.
I will never love myself again.
Who knew then
that someday I would be

thirty-seven, wiping
crumbs off the kitchen table with a sponge, remembering
them, thinking
of this —

those boys still waiting
outside the Stop-N-Go, smoking
cigarettes, growing older.

Guide to Imaginary Places: X-Ray

Through the blue
forest, in the twilight, behind
the white vibration of your bones, a woman
named Marie

carries a glass of water, which glows.

She bears it carefully. She knows

you're broken. The party-
goers are frozen, the music's over. It was

eerie, always, the music, wasn't it? And the flowers
so brief and pale. The beautiful

boys and girls, intangible as song. Who

knew, all along, it could be seen into, or through?
That there were swans
and sails floating
in the lunar dusk inside you?

That the air you breathed
and the water you drank
turned into aria,
and mood?

She knew.

Small Boys Petting Caterpillar

Somewhere, a god
is handling our hearts.
Wonder can kill, accidentally, what it loves.

It's summer. The ditches
are full of fish-scales and glitter. Also
the sepulchre, the tomb, the pit. Someone
has scraped this out of the air

with the dull edge of a knife. Someone

has told them to be gentle, and now
their little hands are light as prayers. If
they breathe, their hands will float away.
The music of dust in water.

One of them is trembling. One

bounces with his legs crossed.
Perhaps he needs to pee.

Above us, on the highest limb, a dangerous piece
of fruit dangles. A teenage
girl is stepping

all over the sunshine in her tennis shoes. Perhaps

that piece of fruit will simply
drift into her hands.
It did, for me. Swiftly,
but with wings.

And the caterpillar

is a word, a soft bit of star. Oblivious, our hearts.
Could that word be *faith,* or *trust,* or is it

some other word which means
to let go in ignorance, or *to hold one's breath and hope?*
And would that word be *love?*

It doesn't matter because
we're helpless in the hands of what does.

The Visibility of Spirits

Those ancients… placed much confidence in the reality of the
spirit-world by which they felt themselves surrounded… Man
believed in an other-worldly order of existence because from
time to time he met its representatives

in his own world. This

morning the breeze is so fresh it's like a knife pulled
cleanly from the center
of a perfectly baked pie. The children

want pancakes for breakfast. *The skillet
is ready,* the Bisquick box says, *when*

*a few drops of water sprinkled on it
dance and disappear.* There is

a flower stuck into
a Diet Coke can on the counter. Or

maybe it's a weed. I plucked her after summer had already

set her on fire with his
blazing rages and ennui. Now

her face is orange, her eye is brown. At

the center of the brownness
there's a sound, a whispered rattle made

out of self-
pity and despair: *It isn't fair.*

Once, lying naked
beside my husband in a sweaty
bed, an awful

moth flew through an open window
and landed on my breast. It

had come from outer space and still
had star-chalk on its face. I felt

so stunned and sure of something
I couldn't wave it away. *Hello? Hello in there I say. Who*

were you, and what happened to you? She looked at me

with her hairy eyes, and seemed to say: I don't

remember, and yet I live, and have
these wings, and for a while, my
girlish figure, my
beauty queen smile. Oh

my God, I said — although
I hadn't taken the Lord's
name in vain
for a long time. And then

Jesus Christ, Jesus Christ, Jesus Christ.

Executioner as Muse

I am Schmidt, who was the son
of a hangman, who
like every other boy
believed for a while that my mind
was the pure white flower of my spine.
I lived. I died. I became

a glimpse of your own face in the window of a train, passing
the barns on fire, the steeples slickened by the rain. I became

a long stripe down the center of the highway
in the middle of the night, leading you into the accident
of someone else's life.

I cannot be buried
because I am always alive.

Like rocks at the bottom of moving water
I have been liberated from my shape — can waver, can climb
the stairs you climb each night,

right behind you stomping
all over the moonlight
in your little silver shoes, locking
the door to your room.

Pick up the pen, and I am you:
Schmidt, the son of a hangman, who
became a hangman, too.

The fruit is ruined, but the bread is baked.
The meat is no longer raw
on its tin plate,

but where
is the hooded cloak
of a warm summer night, the new lover drunk
in the middle of the day, the possum with its
damp white-hearted face? Or the woman

turned to cinders
one morning at the beach. *She*

was a teenager, wearing
a bikini —
who is this? who is this?

There are chalk
drawings on the walls
but they're so crude. What
can they tell us

of what the birds really tasted
when they pierced the pale blossoms
for the first time with their tongues?

The empty church.
The empty school.
The theater, empty, the play is done.

The oven as womb.
The oven as grave.
So much no one
ever needs to say. All

this singing and saying — for centuries — the same.

While inside the oven, not a sound not a sound.
The path leads in, the ashes out.

Green Bicycle

There it is on the horizon, wavering.
There it goes, disappearing, into space.

My father hears sounds in the basement.
He goes downstairs in his underwear, a seventy-
year-old man in the static of night and rain.

The wall's caved in. He turns
and climbs the stairs again.

No trouble, no illumination.
I guess God likes it that way.
But the foundation of my father's
house has collapsed
and the insurance company won't pay
and here we stand this afternoon

stupefied in our wet shoes.

No enemies, no friends.
Without the middle, no beginning or end.
If the phone doesn't ring, if the thing never breaks…

The world says, *Give me*
more of yourself than you can spare
and I'll take you to a strange
city, drop you off downtown, come

to pick you up a little later, greatly changed.

Once, an old man
sat down beside me on a park bench.
He said he was from Ireland.

There were thistles
in the wastefield beside the pond, pre-

historic in their silence, their
shapes, their faith. My bike
was green, and new, and mine. I owned

the most beautiful bike I'd ever seen, and
rode it, watching
myself ride it
like a prepubescent ghost
with long soft hair
into the supermarket's plate-glass window.

It had gotten me to the place
I was, which was, perhaps, farther

than I ever should have been.

He put his hand on my hand, leaned
over and tried to kiss me on the lips.

Oh no, I said — got up, ran, never looked back. But

today I would ask that old man, *What about all that?*

The turtles were paddling on the pond's smooth murk,
poking up their faces for a better look.
The thistles made their hushes
in the breezes. *Tell me, kiss me, Old One. This*

time it'll be
our little secret.

Although, that time, thrilled with my
first horror, riding my bike home
I stopped

over and over to tell this story
to everyone I knew,

and my father, a very young man,
came down there looking for you.

I've never been,
but once I was given a prescription for it
and I still have the pills

in the medicine cabinet, in case.

They say it's always May.
Never any rain —

although the citizens look a little sad
as if they're waiting to be even
happier someday. Don't
bother to ask how it got this way. It's all
roads, crossroads, roadside benches. If you ask

for directions, what can they say?
Only one drunk bus driver
has ever gone and come back.
And he claimed
that time passed very slowly. That

the time it took to wink
at a girl

lasted twenty days. He

couldn't quite remember
its location, but
thought perhaps he'd found it

in a dense forest in Brittany, or
somewhere in central Africa, or

on an extensive peninsula off
the coast of California, discovered

by a Spaniard in 1703.

They're healthy.
They wear crowns. There's

a tree at the center of their town, which
if climbed to the top
is tall enough

for looking back at the rest of the world to see —

nothing but a bit of mountain
pushing out of a bit of ocean, casting

a long, monotonous shadow onto the water

between where we are and where we wanted to be.

My Son in the Cereal Aisle

Today I am one of a hundred mothers
to lose a child at the grocery store.
I am pushing a silver cart piled
high with the gold of the poor.

Weighing grapes. Counting ears of corn.
When I turn around I see

that where the child was standing
by the apples
there isn't anyone, just

a smudged red light, which
rises from them muttering, *how*

large is fear? where do I feel love?

Once, I saw a house cat
at the zoo, caged
with a wild cat, who

paced at the bars, snarling at the babies, while
the house cat yawned in a bit of shade, her
eye a green slit into her mind

and I thought I heard her say, *I'm*

company. If you want to, you can look at me. But

I'm not like this other one,
back and forth, back and forth,
chewing matchsticks, making plans.

Go ahead. The door is open. Thief, come in. I promise
I'll draw this feather
across your throat before I draw the knife.

I leave my cart behind.
Everything packaged.
Everything priced.
The fauna in families. The flora
according to its kind.

Teeth in the grass.
Roses growing in a mine.

The world has come to an end.
Some mothers rise to heaven.
Some claw at the linoleum tiles.
Great bushels of grapes and grain

are dumped into our arms from the sky.

I turn up the cereal aisle

and there I glimpse our children dancing
in and out of the furnace
uninjured by the fire.

Guide to Imaginary Places: Abaton

Never to forget that moment:

We had just stepped out of the plane
and into the air, and the seagulls
were screaming around us, wild

white gloves, demanding
something from us

because we were harmless, alive, and there. Something

entered my heart then, like a curse
or a prayer. I closed my eyes

and cast out a net through which
every other minute
of my life passed.

It was an imaginary net…

It is not an accessible place.

Glimpsed on the horizon, it fills the one who sees it
with sorrow like the vague childhood memory
of linen drying on a line.

Once, the most beautiful blue-eyed cat I'd ever seen
bit my hand with a viciousness
I didn't know beauty had. I bled.

I never
spoke to my mother again
after my mother died. Never even tried…

Sir Thomas Bulfinch said
he saw the outline of it once while
traveling from Glasgow to Troon.

He mentioned a distant music
in his memoirs, music
somewhat like the sun

shining through a thin green leaf

of lettuce in the air, but music

seems unlikely. The name
of the place, in Greek, means

You can't go there.

I stayed in bed for days and watched
a spider in the light spin
an airy web above my head, something

cool and loose, without the use
of force, or weight.

That time, I nearly died

of joy. I was a child. Still alive. Relatives
stood above me, smiling. Summer
was my sickness. Translucent

nurses brought me everything
I needed, while I

swam in and out of sun, which
unraveled its white knitting
on the surface of the pool, and
flew above the orchards, which

stretched in bloom
from my mind to the end of time — just

above the branches, but at great speed, and

I thought I saw a small girl running
like a madwoman beneath the trees.

I didn't even need to eat! I *drank* the beautiful meals
my mother made for me

from coolness and silver spoons. My father

sat at the edge of the bed
and prayed for the angels' protection. Like

talcum powder and masculine sweat, the smell
of wet feathers as I slept. I got better, and

better, listening...

But what was that sound? The clock? The toilet

flushing? Rain on the playground? The ocean
choking on its own waves?

No.

It was a dog
lapping at a bloody tray.

Childhood came and went in a day, and

I woke on Sunday morning in the arms of a stranger.
Oh, I realized then, this

must be joy again. Despite

the headache, the salty thirst, the shame — that

spinning above the bed, more
light than thread, was
exactly, *exactly*, the same.

Spontaneous Human Combustion:
"Girl, Kissing, Bursts into Flames"

It happened to me. I was there. Out

past the factory, where

whole pleasure could be pried
open with an impulse and a wrench. The strange

cowboy of him, chains
and leather and mascara.
I was a keychain, some patchy fog.
The noise of the neural system seemed
to be coming from the stars.

Oh, the wren brought those kisses down from heaven.
A screech owl brought them up from hell.
O earth, wind, water, this

is a simile not satisfied by fire —

Still, if he'd doused me in kerosene that night
I could not have burned better or brighter.

Kitchen Song

The white bowls in the orderly
cupboards filled with nothing.

The sound
of applause in running water.
All those who've drowned in oceans, all
who've drowned in pools, in ponds, the small
family together in the car hit head-on. The pantry

full of lilies, the lobsters scratching to get out of the pot, and

God being pulled across the heavens in a burning car.

The recipes
like confessions.
The confessions like songs.
The sun. The bomb. The white

bowls in the orderly
cupboards filled with blood. *I wanted*

something simple, and domestic. A kitchen song.

They were just driving along. Dad
turned the radio off, and Mom
turned it back on.

SEVEN

from *Fire & Flower*

Alas for the splendor of the prince!

Do Not Leave Baby Unattended

Manufacturer's warning

There is a Maker
who refuses to be sued, a presence
among us which does not wish

to be believed in, or leaned on, or seen.
He drops a small
seed in the earth — fruitful, dutiful, blind —

and it is me. But the earth
around it is also me. He names me
This One's Mother, and there

will never be
any other who could share
a liability. *If anything.*

If something...
The unspeakable lodges itself
like a boiling coin of blood on the tongue.

Even if I die, this one is mine. My faith
is a dove
asleep in the slaughterhouse eaves.

My attention
is a net
sewn of smoke and weight. Even

if I died, my eyes would have to be
always open underground, or blinking
in the sky. Who-

ever you are, up all night
embroidering warnings and disclaimers
on our things, sleep

easy, please. I cannot
sue you, I cannot
even die: Some nights

are darker than trees. The sky
in their hair breathes. There is
no one in this house

when the lights are out
but the great blameless Maker,
and the child,

and the Mother attending these.

Hostess

One of the guests arrives with irises, all

funnel & hood, papery tongues whispering little
rumors in their mouths, and leaves

his white shoes in the doorway
where the others stumble
on the emptiness when they come. He

smiles. He says, "I'm
here to ruin your party, Laura," and he does. The stems

of the irises are too
long and stiff for a vase, and when

I cannot find the scissors, I slice
them off with a knife

while the party waits. Of course, the jokes

are pornographic, and the flowers

tongued and stunted
and seductive, while
in the distance weeds & lightning

make wired anxiety of the night. But I'm

a hostess, a woman who must give
the blessing of forced content, carry
a cage of nervous birds

like conversation through my living room, turning

up the music, dimming
the lights, offering more, or less, or something else

as it seems fit, using
only the intuition
of a lover's tongue, a confessional poet, or
a blind woman fluffing up her hair. It is

an effort, making pleasure, passing
it around on a silver platter, and I'm

distracted all night
by his pale eye

like a symbol of a symbol of something
out of logic's reach forever, until

the soggy cocktail napkin
of my party ends
with this guest carrying
an iris around the kitchen in his teeth, daring me

to take it out with mine. Perhaps

a hostess should not laugh
too hard, or dance
at her own affair. Frolic

is for the guests, who've now
found their coats and shrugged them on. I hear

someone call "Goodnight"
sullenly to the night, disappointment
like a gray fur lining
in her voice. Someone

mentions to this guest
that his shoes have filled with rain, suggests
suggestively he wear
a pair of my
husband's shoes home when he goes. Of course, *of*

course, one of the godmothers has always
come to the christening for revenge. She

leans over the squirming bassinet and smiles
and sprinkles the baby with just
a bit of badness. In his

white smock, he
is prettier than we imagined
he could be, but also
sneaky, easily
bored, annoyed
with the happy
lives of his dull friends. When

he grows up he'll go to parties just
to drink too much, to touch
the women in ways that offer

favors he can't grant. The women

will roll their eyes behind
one another's necks. The men

will bicker about the wine. And
after the party, and the storm, in the after-

quiet, the hostess will find
herself standing
a long time on the patio
alone, as I

stand tonight, in
the still, small song of embarrassment
and regret, Aeolian

in my white dress, the wind

feeling up
those places again, while I
smoke a cigarette, which fills

my whole body with the calm that comes
right after the barn
has burned to the ground, and the farmers' wives
in nightgowns stand around
in moonlit air, their

breasts nearly exposed,
their swan-necks warm. Perhaps

it was the wine. When I
passed him in the hallway by the bathroom, I

thought I heard him say, "Laura, I want

to ruin your life," and, trying to be polite, I said, "That's

fine." I said, "Make yourself at home."

Dear Earth

This is a love note from the sky: All
year I've watched you with my big eye, watched
the muscles in your back as I
stood behind you in the payroll line (those

muscles, are they roads? Could they lead a woman into
the shadows of five o'clock
where she's always wanted to go?). I've

seen you in the parking lot
up to your knees in snow, scraping
the windshield of your white truck, which
spits a riddle of silver thumbtacks

into the silver night. When

you emerge from the Xerox room, I've
seen your conifers
tipped with light. I've

watched you sip
from the watercooler, too, tasting

its cool blue, seen
you pour your coffee
into Styrofoam

until it overflowed.
And this I know:
The view

from here is too removed, diluted
as it is
with flirting & pollution. I want
to fall all over you like a farm, to bless

your fields with weeping, fists
of hail, black
feathers in a frenzy
out of their wrecked nests — simple

gracious rain on your white grapes, or

a holy blizzard of pain: My

tornadoes tearing up your prairies. My

red wind licking its initials in the dust.

The Cause of All My Suffering

My neighbor keeps a box of baby pigs
all winter in her kitchen. They are

motherless, always sleeping, sleepy
creatures of blood & fog, a vapor

of them wraps my house
in gauze, and the windows mist up

with their warm breath, their moist snores. They
watch her peel potatoes, boil

water from the floor, wearing
a steamy gown. She must be like

Demeter to them, but, like this weather
to me, this box of pigs

is the cause of all my suffering. They smell
of invalids, lotioned. Death is over there. When I

look toward my neighbor's house, I see
trouble looking back

at me. Horrible life! Horrible town! I start
to dream their dreams. I dream

my muzzle's pressed
desperately into the whiskered

belly of my dead mother. No
milk there. I dream

I slumber in a cardboard box
in a human kitchen, wishing, while

a woman I don't love
mushes corn for me in a dish. In

every kitchen in the Midwest
there are goddesses & pigs, the sacred

contagion of pity, of giving, of loss. You can't
escape the soft

bellies of your neighbors' calm, the fuzzy
lullabies that drift

in cloudy piglets across their lawns. I dream
my neighbor cuts

one of them open, and stars fall out, and roll
across the floor. It frightens me. I pray

to God to give me
the ability to write

better poems than the poems of those
whom I despise. But

before spring comes, my neighbor's
pigs die in her kitchen

one by one, and I
catch a glimpse of my own face

in the empty collection plate, looking
up at me, hungrily, one

Sunday — pink, and smudged — and ask it
Isn't that enough?

Small, red mitten in the snow —

my heart, my baby, my terror:
At the side of the road in a moment, all of it is there,

although the baby is safe at home, and it isn't

blood or his mitten in this blizzard. Already

in first grade I remember crying, thinking
I am not crying. I'm pretending to cry, while I
watched the other first graders watch me
from the corner of my eye. My crying

was a pack of white wolves
in the woods, beautiful, immutable.

I was a liar, too. I remember

lying and crying at the same time: *He pushed me. He
called me a name!*

So the boy without guilt was sent
to the Office of Invented Crimes. I saw

his white shirttail soaked with nervous sweat
wagging out of his pants as he left — but

who believes a boy?

And even when I left one day
in a blur of accusations
from my first husband, I felt
those wolves in my chest. *I just*

can't take it anymore, I said.

Take what? Take what? he wanted to know, and I
wept into my hands, pretending, although —

in truth — I wanted nothing from him. I wanted

only to be pure of him, and never

to have felt
what I felt
about him, just

imagined the camera on me, what
my suffering would look like
from the distance of God

to a girl. For decades, the days were long
and full of stars. The nights were brief and false. I
couldn't
imagine what love was, what

fear meant, and didn't care. But now

I see this blood-spot, heart-stop
of a baby's mitten in snow and all of it is there in

a moment at the side of the road —
authentic, and primitive,
the terror like love, the love like terror — and wonder

where did that girl go, and wonder

who will punish her for what she wasn't
now that I'm a mother?

Confections

Caramel is sugar burnt

to syrup in a pan. Chaos

is a pinch of joy, a bit of screaming. An infant sleeping's
a milky sea. A star

is fire & flower. Divinity
is beaten out of egg whites

into cool white peaks. Friendship

begins and ends in suspicion, unless
it ends in death. Ignite

a glass of brandy in a pan, and you'll

have cherries jubilee: sex
without love's sodden nightgown

before your house burns down. Music's

a bomb of feathers
in the air
in the moment before it explodes
and settles itself whispering
onto the sleeves of a child's choir robe. And

a candied apple's
like a heartache — exactly

like a heartache — something
sweet and red tortured to death

with something sweeter, and more red.

Will the trees remember what happened in the shade
when the U-Haul passes the graveyard
and this is turned to wind?

Dear God, I've stood
in my own path
and passed myself as I passed, and caught

a glimpse of my own face catching a glimpse of me.

Dear God, if you are God, is that

what God is? *I have stood*

in my path as I passed, and my name

was a mystery whispered to the wind. Dear God, if

there is a god, where
is that woman now? The one

in the U-Haul, the one in the grave, the one

driven by hounds
past her own home, the one

who was a secret to herself, naked
in the shade? In the language

of her century, she'd pray, with a heart

full of thorns, in a forest
full of corpses, in the screaming

confession of peacocks in trees — the seconds

of her life scattered
like the little knife-blades of fishes in the shallows, in
the conscious hours

watching their own loss: I

have passed that woman passing, God, and

I want to believe
her passing was a prayer — all along, all along

whether or not you were there.

Dear Water

I am your lost daughter and, as always, you

are listening & fish. Though

I sift you for sunlight, it
runs from me in glistening pins, vanishes

in the wavering map

of your ungraspable heart. When I

reach in, you

swallow my cold hands again, swallow

the joy they'd hold — that foil-gold, which

plates the shadows like damage
done, where

the trees project their dreams

on the drifting surface of your sleep, and

the reeds are fleeting & green.

What I Hear in Your Hair

upon Jack's first haircut

Somewhere there's an office
in which a secretary sits at a desk.
Her task is to suppress

the names of the dead. The machine

she feeds makes the music
of stars over traffic, the radio
noise of the sky, the static

of lived-up lives — *placenta & ashes & air.*

She shreds them into thin
white filaments of light, which grow

longer and thinner, drift
and sway in the sky, like

electric beach grass, blown, while
the mechanical teeth of her

machines whir even
at night — the music
of mowers, mowing time. It's

so hard to forget, to keep

them off our lips, to erase
what we called them, and the way

their plain faces
turned toward the sound of
what they thought were their names. But

a few things must
be left behind each hour — *placenta*
and ashes — and there's the sound

of cats lapping water
from vases of daisies
as we put these things away

to make room for the newly born, the infants
who descend upon us
newly, wanting
to be called something, wanting
to have a few

original things to say — these

babies like naked fruit with human skin
expanding in our midst. Therefore

an office exists, quite simply, for this, and

a secretary sits
at a desk, doing
what she does simply. Still, before I pass

these scissors carefully there, I bend
to kiss your head, and hear

their names whispered in your hair.

A Long Commute

Faith is a long commute. Lots
of time to change
the station on the radio, time
to relive the past, to consider

the future the way
the boy in the bus station
standing by the trashcan
the afternoon the bomb went off
must have had time to consider

his own hands carefully in his hands. The road

is narrow and it goes

straight through the gardens of Paradise. Lots

of soggy godhearts dripping
blood on their bloody vines. Behind me

a beautiful blind girl carries a Bible
home in a plastic bag, while

before me, an old
woman and her old mother
drive a Cadillac over
the flowers slowly.

Barney

I love you. You love me.

He is the true Zero in his cap & bells, in the terrible
lizard of his skin. I see him

crossing the tundra in snowshoes like a big
hug coming, lost

on Earth
in a body. Consider: if I become him

what kind of suffering? This
afflicted creature, dancing

for the hostile, costumed. Venus

loves him. He loves me, has given

himself to the whole world without
mortification, given
himself to the landscape

of sap and snow and cloud, come

unto the world
and made it pregnant, singing
to the invisible family before him, swallowing

the sorrow of children — innocent, curious, extinct.
A narrow stream of tears runs right through him.

When the beloved
is in everyone, in the excited
imbecile, the timid

orgy of sleep, who
can help but think of Christ
with his sandals & lambs? Why

all of us? Why not just some? Oh
the emptiness of so much. The everlastingness. This
hug. Quivering, endured. A purple
balloon like our hearts, naked
and blown up

without flesh, wrinkles, fur. It loves
without an object of it, and how
we long to keep

the beast of it
stuffed down inside us

along with the little saints & fools
who sing pitiful songs in our chests.

Dear Fire

Every night my father dreams he golfs in hell
with you. The woods
lick the sky

above my father's game
with flames, and he

is trapped alive
for eternity in the place
where his hope starts
and his patience ends, losing

his ball in the burning
thickets again and again — the burning

thickets into which
everything we hurry through

in this life is lost. When

my father wakes, the grass
is sweet and long with spring. The sprinkler

whirls across the street, and the leaves
fall like cool
compresses out of the trees. But even

then you're there. Pennies

on his dresser, his hot pockets
empty of copper. He

shaves too fast, and trickle of his blood boils
luxuriant as a woman's
red hair down the drain. My

father drinks his coffee
at the kitchen window, pacing, while
the red face of a geranium strains

its brain toward the sun, blooms
its aneurysm, waiting, shouts

Fire! in the crowd, which

surges as one body of vivid oxygen
against the microwave's jammed door.

Burial

Where my father has retired, there's so much sand
he can only grow

a small, crooked
carrot in the ground. It tastes

like a finger, or it tastes like the sound
a song makes passing
through a rabbit hole. My father has stepped

off the porch
of his mailman's life
into a stinging wind, which

pushes the dunes a little farther
every year, butter-

knives them closer
to the town, until

there's sand every morning
on my father's toast, the grainy *hello*
of time on his teeth.

When I was a child
I choked one day
on a circle of cinnamon candy I'd

already sucked to glass beneath
my tongue's red scrap. I

stopped breathing
for a while
and in that place

the breathless wait for death, I

heard a train's brakes gouge two
melon-smiles in the sky. An old

woman laughed, then
spat in my eye, and

although I was only a child, I
understood that I would die. I
could understand

that the whole world
was just my breath, and

that, without it, the whole
world was going to end.

Instead, my father
came up behind me, and
slapped me hard and fast on the back.

Infants' Corner

Little lambs and angels softened, all

their wings and features blended

by the weather

into a murmurous
world, murmuring
typhus, diphtheria, flu, the way

long sleep mollifies a face, slips
a gentle mask of dough

over its angles and planes. I used

to walk among those names

of babies
in their graves: *Samuel, Sarah, Vaughn.*

The vowels like yawns. All

those damp lambs down there snuffling
eternity calmly
out of the fur of the dirt. A warm

fleece of them would rise
from the lawn, smell

of rheumy lace, sodden
nursery drapes, while

the earth above them lung'd
its smallpox song, shed

tears that fogged the churchyard
under the eye of God, while

fever, long forgotten, walked among them

like a woman wearing
scarlet gloves, humming
a lullaby
in the contagious rain, the rain, which
blurred and muffled everything. Time

& weather, weather & time

seemed to make
soap of pain. But she

was still a stranger in that place, a tourist
among the loved. She

liked the one that said, *Wipe
your tears and weep no more, Little*

John has gone before — so
maudlin in its longing, like a drunk

stumbling through a liquor store
where they won't sell him any
liquor anymore. She

knew nothing yet about
the awfulness of love, the hot-
washcloth stars that fall
all over the world
when an infant turns, bawling

in your arms, the steam

of yellow sickness in a cup, or

the dream of them still calling
for comfort, milk, or Mother
underground — the sweet

and sorrowful shoes
on their small feet, or how

some kinds of grief should shame us

long after their mothers are gone.

I saw you in the Laundromat — my love, my voice, my empty
dove.
I saw you in the closet in

the emptiness of shoes. I saw you in the window and saw myself
in you — *my*

honeycomb, my fate, brief
virgin I once was. All

summer, white grapes

spun themselves from sun
and water on their vines —

incandescent thumbs, clear-

blooded and alive. Love

made love to me the way
a spider shrouds a fly
in silk and lies until

he's amorous
and quiet
as a meal. And now I know that love like that is nothing, but
bottomless as
the space contained

by the gold hoop of a wedding ring
lost one day in linens: Five

thousand brides could dance
at one time
on that bright dime. Christ's

white tigers, flying

through hoops of fire. *You*

did not see me, but I saw you. Thief: Womb: Vowel

wrapped in light like
an old woman's
faded hair.

As in heaven, I saw you there, and all I could do was stare
dumbly as you tumbled

your stars & flowers with my towels.

Fire & Flower

Nights, he'd climb
the fire escape to me. The sky

was rocket-fire. Rain was my fire crying. Now

I sleep beside a child. Song of a million years. Song

of milk & mouths turned to white blossoms
in walled gardens.

Sleep, like a swan boat drifting

down a bowery stream. Long

feathers on the water in our bed's unfolding flower.

EIGHT

from *What It Wasn't*

How that time has passed away...

There are the plaster stars, the dew's

slow mucilage
in the garden, and God

spreads Himself across the heavens

without form. All

that smeared star froth pads
the moon in cotton, a doughy

opal, a Peeping Tom's
featureless face at the window

glowing, while

shed bandages of fog, bacterial
and womanish, rise
from the lawn

when she takes her girdle off.

Cocktail Waitress

Things change, but those days
my tray was always full

of damp blue veils, amazing

scarves of waste-things washed
up gasping between the waves
as I ran into the future with them, the way

a child might run toward her mother
with wet hair like weeds
sopping in her hands
one morning at the beach. I still believed

the day would come
when I would bump straight into love
in a barroom, like
a businessman with wings. Later

I'd loosen his red noose
in a mildewed room
of the Holiday Inn, un-
button his stiff shirt

and there those wings would be, soft
and alive, two

wet white hens, cool
or clammy
under my hands. Half

skin, half
tissue paper smelling
like fresh and restless paste. They'd

tense and tremble
when I touched them, stunted

gulls with nowhere
to go, while my
fishnet stockings, strung
up, dripped
above the tub. But my

father called my roommates
the False Hope Club. Five
ephemeral station wagons idling, five
lilacs browning

on the sidewalk, five
unsolved murders just
waiting to occur. We

lounged around in lipstick while the sky
rippled its
blue metallic dime-store slips outside, while

the heiress starved to death below us, and the thin
blondes above us made a feast
of water every night
by their TV. Once
we found a life-sized plastic doll

strung up behind our Dumpster, like
a sacrifice to nothing, dagger

through her heart, and down the block

a muddy set of women's
underwear was found
beneath some cardboard in a barn. My

father thought it was a warning
from our landlord, but I
still believed in miracles
and spirits of every kind, believed
one day I'd find a man who'd pant
and struggle

in a victory garden — mine —
snagged in vegetation, coiled

vines around his wrists. His
lush hair would be bleached
green, and there might even be

pumpkins swollen like awful
god-heads at his feet, or
overgrown suns — while my

figment fell and rose around him, a foil
screen, while my

melancholy figment
sipped a margarita

and filed her fingernails to speartips

in the future by his pool.

Childhood Visions of Beautiful Women

They steal across the swamps
with bare feet
and green wings, not

dead, and not asleep, not
starfish, earthworm, fern — singing

Ivy growing on a stone,
Ivy growing on the earth,
Ivy growing on a stone on earth.

Scummed and purring, the swamps
are full of motherwort
and loosestrife

as they always were, while

back home, another woman wavers
in the kitchen's hallowed light, wearing

slippers in the middle
of the night. She

sings a song from far away — a song
from somewhere in between

grace and the strange veiled rays
of the microwave —

Lichen growing on a birch,
Lichen growing on a church,
Lichen growing on the Virgin's marble robes.

Roxy's Bordello, Boarded Up

It was never much more than a trailer, a barracks, a row
of old beds and feathered pillows

sunk into night
and memory like

a long boat on a dark ocean, or

a bird in mud. Just

a thin mattress, here and there, a dark-
haired girl with a lisp. The wind

whistles ditties
through its loose teeth, *She*

who has no husband now, will never have one. She

who calls her child
by another child's name
will stand without shoes a whole life
in a neighborhood of riddles, failure, blame. There's

the sound of a sweatshop somewhere — that
dull foot-thump
of murky servant girls working

eternally underground, while

the first night of winter travels toward us
wondrously cold, dressed
in a gown
of viruses

and phlegm. Oh —

the whore who doesn't die
gets old and stands alone
on the deck of a vessel that's circled

with ghost-white birds that beat

a blur of white-gloved hands
and gull-black blood. Tonight

her sinking ship is strung
with ornamental lights, or

Christian martyrs' names — their

dim faces
snuffed flames.

Andy's Lanes & Lounge

On the night of the miracle cure.
On the evening of the electric chair

I am twirling on a barstool. Some-
one shouts STRIKE. A girl
shrieks. There's
waste and loneliness in public places, and

the moon hangs candy-red
above the watery world where
the terrorists have just discovered
the weapon that will kill us

all — a handful
of nightfall
tucked inside a bowling ball. There

will be squealing when it shreds us, and
the moon tonight is red as something

too sweet and full of female screams to eat.

———————————————————————

On the night of the miracle cure.
On the evening of the electric chair

the man they execute
lives — although his white hair
turns dove gray, although
his red hair smokes. And

the old lady they've left
naked and embalmed on a table

licks her fingertips, which
still taste like flue, stainless

steel, sugarwater, sweet as youth.

God I've never been less hopeless

and the bitters have never tasted
more like kisses, and

the maraschino cherry is so
syrupy and bright
I have to hold it in my mouth
and close my eyes before I bite.

Woman in a Girdle

(Overgrown Garden)

Afternoon wilts, the way
lungwort withers in hot weather, its

silver-spotted leaves gone
soggy and tubercular
sucking summer out of the ground.

———————————————————

(Lazy Susan)

The cat's tail sweeps the floor
while the dishes are washed

by the dirt. Now, all
over the suburb she can hear
the sweaty, stucco walls
of the human houses breathe
like cheese, and she
remembers seeing
the World's Smallest Horse

at the Lubbock Fair, circling

its own shit
at one end
of a big pen.
In its

small saddle, it

was so, so small.

(Nap)

The shepherd on the hillside
cannot keep the flock together.
The sun's been boiled to something pale

and flaccid as a dumpling. The

shepherd stumbles among them, but there's
so much yeasty light that he
can no longer tell

the sheep from the sky, which hangs
above the world, a woolly scarf.

(Dinner)

How skinny the Cornish hen
appears in the oven.
A plucked, baked, feminine
fist. Meal

for a prisoner
in a wide prison cell. Bald
mouse in the lion's cage.
While —

dusk wraps itself around her
like a loose, blue cave.

What It Wasn't

On January 1, 1976, Tracey Lawson, 11, and her cousin were playing in
a backyard five miles south of Harlingen, Texas. As they looked out on a
plowed field beyond the yard, they saw a black bird of extraordinary size:
over five feet tall. Its wings were folded around its body, and the bird was
staring at the girls through large, dark-red eyes. Its head was bald, and it
had a beak at least six inches long.

It wasn't night: We
knew everything there was to know
already about night, how

night is a small wool cake
of rodent bones, how

an owl can choke it up like
wisdom, or a tooth. We

were virgins, still, and cousins

so it wasn't about sex.
And it also wasn't death, like

the handfuls
of jackdaws
that every winter tossed themselves

down the hopeless chimney, head-
long into the cozy
hell of our woodstove. Even

the Stealth Bomber
would certainly have made
a dark new wind
with its bat wings. But this

didn't whistle

and it wasn't maimed. It wasn't

Mary, or the Air Force, or your brother Jim. Too

young yet to want
the government's attention
or the sympathy of cops, we

weren't mad, and we'd never heard
about the netherworld, worm-

wood, pharmaceuticals, vermouth. This

wasn't the realm
of darkened sun, or
the unanticipated outcome
of sublimated lust, and we

were not the only ones: Two

men in Brownsville saw it
first, saw it
settle on a patio near a cooler

of brand-new beers. This
thing certainly

was not no neighbor's pet, this
ugly, tarred & feathered angel. They

claimed it lunged

but didn't bite, that
it was not a Jungian symbol
of any type, not

even a symbol
of the dangerous action
of instincts upon
the drunken man. It never

crossed their minds
to shoot, or throw a rock, and only

three hours later it had winged
its way to us. And no

it was no whistler, I'll
grant it that, or
a wheezer, and, indeed, it did

not try to bite. Although

after that
the vacant valley, it
looked more vacant
than it ever had:

Clearly
a symptom
of dissolution, that

restless, indeterminate, ab-

straction of discontent. To some
it comes as tedium, a tepid
Calgon tub of tedium, the yuppie

flu, the dull dawn you wonder whether
you ever loved your husband, why
you ever moved to the suburbs. But

we were only children, and to us

this thing occurred early, as
a man-sized bird. It

didn't smell, but
if it smelled at all it would have smelled
like useless fashion boots. It *was*

sullen I'll admit, and always
a little drunk by supper, but

it never shattered families

or ended in divorce. It never
abused the power
it never wanted to have. It never

murdered, packed, or moved. What-
ever it was, it was

never what it was, not
even a shadow
of its former bird. Just

the sudden knowledge that
we'd been children once, full
of futures, and

we no longer were.

WARNING:

Here they've hacked some
poor smoker into steaks
and made us a slide-
show of his lungs. The tile

in the bathroom
of the community college
is cold, and there's

a chaos of faces before I faint
and the dull bell of my head on the floor
summons the smoking

dead from their graves: the corrugated
lungs of my uncles, the creamy
corpse-eyes of my aunts, and

the earth falls apart like dirt as I
try to hold my own
crumbling chest together.

A girl runs to get my husband, who's
having a cigarette outside. *We*

have to quit, I tell him
on the car ride home

and I show him the message
from the Surgeon General
as I smack the last one
out of the pack.

The first day passes so slow
we can feel our hair

grow, even
under our arms, our eye-
lashes even. Then

the elementary school
where we were students burns
to the ground, just
some rags left flapping
on the flagpole, nostrils

and ashes, steaming
volcanoes, and the message
a dead bird brings us
as it falls at our feet
in a soggy ball.
Before

we go to bed I rip
my underwear off. Someone's
poisoned my black bra
and my torso
has turned
to roast beef. I hear

my husband grind his teeth
all night in sleep

and in the morning, when he
rolls over in bed
to smile at me, the
teeth are gone, just
a bloody smithereen left

hanging from his gums, a molar

on his pillow. We

choose our plots that same day
at the Catholic
cemetery — two
together
just beyond
the chain-link fence, where

the suicides are buried

beside the musicians.

Sad Song

There are women
carrying torches
coming toward us. Their

eyes are accidents. The kinds
that happen on the highway
in the middle of the night. The kind

we glimpse as we drive by. A flare
in snow, a metal cage
with ruined tigers in it. We

look away, and then we're home. There

are hundreds of women marching forward, carrying
torches like a burning orchard. They're
coming for us, and everything's on fire. Even

the torpedo boats. Even the starfish creeping along
the ocean floor in families, in

the utterly deaf and dumb. Here

they come: You

open your mouth, and I
see the word *bye*
float out, like
a jeweled wasp with
a golden Y around her neck. Those

wasps have made
an elaborate nest
in the attic, in

my trunk of party dresses: All
that buzzing about you, all
that frantic dancing

like a barbed breeze in my hair. I

lift the lid of that trunk
for the first time in years. Stale

carnations and yellow lace. All
the invitations I didn't take, turned
to female dust. *I'll*

always love you, I say, and you
wince a bit, like Zeus, who
didn't know he had

an armored woman in his head. Those

women wait
with their torches on the porch, but when
I step outside to take
my own flaming place, they

turn suddenly to stone, like
all the marble madonnas, trapped
and standing
on Saturday

at the empty art museum. Their

long medieval shadows drape the floor like
loose blue cloaks: Look

carefully under the veil
of one of those — the one

who has been waiting at His tomb
for seven hundred years: If

you hold your breath you'll see
she's grieving
with a sly, white smile. Perhaps

that one's only posing
as a stone. Maybe she's

just as alive as the garden hose, coiled
and breathing in the dank
dark of the garden shed. Perhaps

she's held her stone breath
a long, long time. The way
some moths, sensing nets, will

fold their wings in half
and seem to the untrained eye to be
just a few more brown and withered leaves

clinging to the tree. But

they're not: If

you sing a sad song loud enough, the boys
on those torpedo boats
can hear you under the sea.

Recollection

During one of Wilder Penfield's operations, the right temporal lobe of a
woman was exposed and electrically stimulated. The woman was fully con-
scious and described her sensations. The recollection of a mother calling
her child was evoked, and that of a carnival.

I was that mother one dust-gray drunk
and ugly summer. I had

a picket fence   a violent husband   several
housewife friends with wine. At night

the carnival lit up a swollen
lip of distant sky   like
electric teeth on every side
of a dark, dry tongue. It was

as if the child's name I called that night could scorch

an orchid   or an onion
out of conscious
or unconscious earth   all

white light and lightbulb sprouting
tangled arms underground. Summer

was green
with green and pumping blood. *Another*

woman's un-
remembered memory: All

that time, that's all I was. So

many years passed her by   stiff
as dreaming cows   while I

just turned to some-
thing glimpsed once
on a long dull drive through dust. But

that's the drive we all make once
into the temporal center of
our own lost lives. *It*

was summer in the cornfield in the backseat
of a dark car   as it sifted the smell of soft rot   old

blankets soaked in fever sweat tossed
across our dreams. There might have been

cold steam and change all spring   writhing
like orchid bulbs under our feet   the way

a vivid high school girl-
friend's un-
remembered maiden name might
swim to the murky

surface of the pond
on a rainy summer day. *Amnesia*

Paramnesia   Oblivescence   Fugue   and

another woman's life
simply rises from the right
temporal lobe of the open
mind   moist
and encephalitic as

some cool fish eye silver-spooned
out of a thin, gray soup:

Maggie   Mary Gail   Sweethearts, come back:

Witness

the strange kind wildness of the brain   how

it will always open
its hungry mouth
one last time
to let the children out.

The August air has turned to blurred fur, all
flesh, paste, sponge, sprawled

wool on the humid hills. When

she puts the girdle on, there is the sound

of panting sheep, the sound

of sloppy, tropical fruit sloshing
warm and milky juice beneath its skin.

NINE

from *Housekeeping in a Dream*

...dark under the cover of night...

House Fable

There were always human handprints
on the walls, honey-

pawed in the kitchen, bloodred
in the bedroom: a house

built on snow, beaten
and teased and fed fish. The dog

dozed by the fire, breathed
orange dust from his nostrils and spat

out colored dirt. Behind the hearth
two children (the kidneys)

played with a pretty box; an old man (the head) slept
near them in a chair, and a young

married couple (the intestines) stood
kissing at the window. Out-

side, the valley was wandered with reindeer. Spring
came and the stairs

and orchid bulbs
ascended to nothing but sky. The clover

hid like hornets in the garden
beneath an enormous rock. *Grease*

*flour   feathers   in the kitchen
and in the parlor the chiming of clocks. Some-

thing suckled, something starved. A sled
in the attic, and a waterfall

etched in an ashtray. *Send
word*   soft-penciled in Russian

on the back of a postcard
of two old ladies in black standing

bent before a blurred gray fence: our
great-aunts Dominance

and Submission, who died
at one another's hands.

Tribe of Women

I spent one whole spring day with my sisters

in a departed garden
in a foreign land. *Please*

was the word we used
to disagree with one another. Then

that one had to go and get the baby, who'd
gotten ahold of a ladder and dragged it
through the tulips, fallen

forward like frightened women
stripped of their fancy skirts. *Oh*

no the gardener said, but I

said *Sweetheart,* being
godmother to that child
and every night I told her
old wives' tales
before she closed her eyes.

I palmed the baby's belly while she teethed
a bleeding piece of fruit. *Here*

is the basement
where they shot
the Czar's daughters
and their little dog. More

jam, more crackers, more
dainty cakes
upon a little table

while the milky trillium screamed
all over these mountains for miles. Even

the baby was sick with desire. *Papa*
she said to Beethoven's bust. *Papa*
to the crucified scarecrow.

And the salmon slapped
the river like spoons, *and a cow*
jumped over the moon. Here

is the perfect garden, I said, here
the ballerinas
never need to eat. *Oh*

please the feminist said
and the psychic told my fortune
by reading an arrangement of eggs.
And one of our sisters was dark and perhaps

a bit suicidal, too. All
day she plucked a crow
that sang *how long? how long?*
Though she also loved her tea
and drank it extra-
sweet
and planned to hang herself
one day from the cherry tree

when it was not in bloom.

But it was always in bloom.
And the logs rolled limb-
less down the river
and the waves went back and forth at our door
and the ponies followed each other

in weak circles
on the church lawn

and one of us might have been having
an affair with her husband's brother. She
painted her toenails mother-
of-pearl, while the baby was just a bright

package of laughter
in the grass, and the soldiers
were glad

and drunk
when they finally stumbled upon us.
First, they shot our horses. Then
they grunted above us

for hours in their animal trances.

Sweetheart: someone wrote it
in blood on the wall of her cell.

Crow's Feet

They've found where the universe ends, and it ends
in a wall, a hedge, a pan
of dishsoap soaking
in a greasy sky, though

some of the bubbles are more
than sixty million light-years long. Some of the bubbles are swans

feasting on cold white peas beneath
the delicate worry of willows, the blisters weeping on your high-heeled feet.
        And finally you're left
    with nothing
more than a knickknack shelf, a row

of china cups
that belonged to your mother, who was

insomnia itself, and damselflies
hatching in still water. One

of the cups is so
fragile it cracks its white
flowers to ash under only
the duster's pink feather-hover. Though

one of them will never break at all. You
throw it again
and again at the wall.

Babysitter

for Antonya Nelson

When I was sixteen I decided
to eat the underworld fruit.
What the hell, I said.
It was juicy, and cold.

My hair was black so I dyed it
black, and I wore
nothing but black.
I still have the skull
tattooed on my ass. I never cried
and I never laughed. I decided

to reinvent silence
right in my own home.
My father's hair went white overnight
and he hung up his mailman blues
and retired. My mother
fell down the stairs and died.
My father said he was glad
at least she couldn't see
what would become of me.

That winter I divided
the bear arrows up
among my friends. *Aim*
to kill, I said
and I tacked its head
to the post of my bed. At night
it sang its grizzly song
to me, and I slipped
my neck between its teeth.
I trust you completely,
I said.

For attention at school
I swallowed fire, I ate
crows whole, and once
I jumped out
from behind a bush
and scared a priest to death.

At sixteen I discovered sex
in the backseat
of a cannibal's car, though
we only went so far.
It was my first taste
of human flesh, and it
was tender and sweet.

When I was sixteen, the beast
came looking for me, some
of my friends impaled themselves
on rusty knives, while I
was granted eternal life,
I don't know why. Wild
dogs followed me home, rabid
bats ate

from my hand, and children —
children loved me.

At night while you were out dancing
your children gathered around me
and put their little
raccoon hands in mine.

Parrot, Fever

                                        Laura

my first lover taught his parrot to say.   *Laura*

it lurched from foot to foot
in its ecstatic mask, mocking
my dull body
with its painted wings. The sky

was pallid and naked above
its green and tangerine.   *Laura*

it rasped frantic, the way
a mother calls her homely child, my name
on its black tongue long

after my lover
had forgotten what it was. The ringed

fluff around its neck
ruffled as it watched us with its stiff
sarcastic eye, beady
eye of the hunted, sneer
of the terribly depressed. *They go mad*
when they're alone
a pet shop owner told me, later, over
a dozy, slumped sick one he couldn't sell.
In Australia

four thousand
might gather in a day
when the trees are dripping nectar. They might

grow drunk
and unable to fly, wander in circles, feathers
plastered with pollen, controlled

free fall, psychedelic blitz. But his

finger-tame bird would sometimes whir
blind around the apartment, bumping
the beige walls   a gaudy
moth, mutant

and chattering, utterly
insane. *Who's*

a pretty bird? it begged. *Who's Laura, Laura?*

And even Sparkie, the famous
fifties radio & TV bird, who knew
383 sentences, uttered the last words *Love*

you Mama before he fell
from his perch face-
first into the sixties
newsprint at the bottom of his cage. His

owner claimed he knew
what each of his words meant. *Yes*
he said when he was pleased, *gentle*
when he was touched, even

his high-pitched screams, even
when he mimicked
the dripping tap, the whistle
of bombs on London. What

thought can exist
without words? All

owners beg us to see: What

words can exist without thought.   *Brief*

I understood all along   *Love you*
hallucinatory *Mama:* Years

later I saw
his best friend in a bar, and
he told me the bird was still saying my name, until
my lover married a beautiful, jealous
woman who gave it away. I laughed

long and hard about that, spectacular
grief I never knew I had, like a cage

of tropical birds in the middle
of a mall
in the Midwest, their clatter
battering the cinder-block walls
behind a rack of expensive dresses.   *Who's*

a pretty bird?   Perhaps
it expected to hear its name
but I never asked
what it was. Like all

exotic things

I just imagined it would end cat-
ravaged, stuffed, or diseased. *Breast
cancer, parrot fever, a feathered hat,* I said.

One of them will never break at all. You
throw it again
and again at the wall, and time

rises all around you. A sticky fog. The sleepy Sirens in the fountain nod
        and nod but never sleep. It seems
the water that spills on their smooth feet
is endless, and green, but it's always

the same water splashing marble, over
and over, and the sound of it is nothing
in the lost child's ear: That

child was conceived as a scheme, a plan, a last-
ditch effort, which is nearly
the same as the sexual mistake
your own mother made: Your

body was a thing your mother imagined
in which the past could be contained. You

were no more or less than an afternoon. A place. Your name-
less father's face rising
and falling above
a small white bed. And lost forever
in those cool sheets — a girl's
silver bracelet
of DNA.

God exists. Instead
we are a group of teenage girls, drunk
at one of those awful
carnivals in a field, out
between the airport and the mall.
It's raining, and this
has become a festival
of mud, which is just
fine with us. A man

with hundreds of tattoos
has taken a fancy to Heidi
and is slipping her extra darts
to lob at the balloons. There are sirens
every time she misses, and she wins
nothing. Why

is there straw in the mud, why
is it plastered now to the wet
sleeves of our leather jackets? Something
cruises into the air
with its lightbulbs zapping
and when we turn around, the man

has disappeared with Heidi. Am I wrong
or has every teenage girl been
at this same carnival in rain, in 19-
78, with four wild friends and a fifth of peach
schnapps in her purse with its bit
of rawhide fringe? Music

spins at us and away from us
as the Octopus starts up
its scrambling disco dance. Am I

the one who says *Don't worry*
she'll be back or have I
gone to the port-o-potty
to barf again by now? Imagine

hours later
when we are terrified and sober and
still waiting, when she
reappears with her hand
tucked into the back
pocket of the tattooed man
who has no T-shirt on now under
his black vinyl vest
so we can see all
his swastikas and naked
ladies — imagine

that we are just
a few peasant girls
on a hill in Portugal. It's night, but the sun's

swung out of the sky
like a wrecking ball on fire
and even the skinny whores

in their ice-cold brothel smile
while the Fascists are gripped
with cramps
and shudder in their shiny
uniforms with tassels. Imagine
when we see Heidi:

her blurred blue robes
in the distance, her soft
virgin voice, and the way
it knocks us to our knees

like a crate of fruit, tossed
off a truck
and smashing into the street.

A girl's silver bracelet
of DNA, and you

emerged much bigger than a bird
so your mother built a female nest
from whore's hair, bric-a-brac, and vacuum cleaner ash. At night

she wore the clammy cold-cream that was once
her own mother's vanity
and grief.
So what? she says, but you know
it's not what she means: *A few*

lines around your eyes, get
used to it or die. But the crows
are larger than you

and they have voices that sew stitches
and zippers across the sky.

Ravine

At night we crawled out of our windows
with our parents' bottles while they
were drunk and locked in combat. Dogs

would strain their chains at the stars
and the smell of girls' underwear
in backyards as we shuffled
over the summer stumps
of suburban grass. We wore

our hair orange
in those days, ugly
and amazing as grace. We talked
on and on about boys
as if we knew one, and now

I bleed with nostalgia
to think of that, the wet
banks of the ravine
where we slid down to drink, just

two girls getting
immaterial on wine, maybe

smoking if we had one, sucking
the kitchen lights in the distance down
like a smoldering forest of pines.

The heart
named us sisters
with its dull thumping. I loved her

with pain like handfuls of ice. She
loved me enough to let me

go on and on as no one
ever has
about my body parts, my
optimistic theories
about development and growth
while we were in the bubbling
test tube of it. Sometimes

we might lift
our arms up and sing
while the moon trampled us with green
light. Mindless —

we were that young
and in the little light we got, once
or twice we found
in that damp slash evidence
that other life existed: a milky rubber

dried-up and openmouthed
as a baby bird, hauled
out of a nest to its death
by gravity
and wind, thinking

as it shriveled, bald
and wet through air, that
at least it knew what flight
would be like
if it had feathers to do it.

We poked it up with a stick
and whipped it into the air.
It thrilled us as much
as sex ever would, as if
something had shed
its better skin in our path.

Exploding Homes

She says, *Some mornings I hear music*
coming from my own home
and wonder if I should go in yet or wait
with my luggage on the porch
until the dancing's done. But that's
always how it is
to return from the dead
or after the divorce, to descend
in a raincloud or to rise
in a ball of fire: To come back to say hello
with roses at first and then with weeds, to
see your own grave grown over
and your home exploded. *Far*
into the forest a man
kept a pretty daughter in a trailer. He
drove her to work at Woolworth's every morning. She
is, of course, the one who arranges the square
blue scarves there
in a glossy corner of Apparel
to this day. To this day
they don't know how the old man
and the trailer caught on fire. Someone
heard singing at the center of the flames. *So many*
scarves to arrange. So much
weight to be gained. "There
are homes that just explode," one fireman says. And
there are also large discount department
stores, we know, in which
wide-eyed girls place lambskin gloves in rows
on sale tables — without
any hands in them: There
are sorrowful racks of black pants beside
whole dull families of brightly

colored felt coats, laughing. One
coat is a man's. One is a woman's.
One will belong to their child.

Before we're born our fathers' cars have fins.
Our mothers watch them from the riverbank hatching
into the air like a quick
gas of mites: They rise

all at once, earth-
like out of the water gone
prismatic with tears, tanker oil
and plastic sandwich wrap. Our mothers are wearing
saddle

shoes and pedal pushers: This
is not yet Planet Sex, but soon

we will be born, sons
and daughters of the sixties: Little
tinfoil minnows, and the morning will make a delicate pleasure
of bird lungs on our lips. And then

our fathers' cars will evolve
into long blue Fords. Prussian and dragging
their rusty mufflers
behind them like old tails, sparking

the night's dark road: We'll
eat deviled ham and Wonder Bread and thrive, and down-
town will die: Our new
landscape clatters in the future
like big white knives
on a giant's platter. Else-

where there's a Buddha, and he smiles — a fat
and happy child, but our
Christ will writhe
in agony on a wall. He

curses the body, the jacks & ball, the vinyl couch, and all
of material time as it stretches ahead, a tide
of diapers and Twinkies rising
over the rest of his American life, until

they build the Mall — *that long white tunnel of light, we'll see*
our mothers waiting for us
at the end of it when we die. Grand

Rapids is a jewel by 1972, a diamond
ring from which the stone has slipped
on someone's honeymoon, or
a small gold horse
with no jade eye. *Conquest of the Planet*

of the Apes will play all summer, here
in the cradle
of civilization, while the moon wanes
and waxes above
the sticky parking-lot tar, above

the Tigris and Euphrates. The Nile, the Po, the Rhine. The stars

grow fainter and fainter
in artificial light: The fears
and hopes
of the tribe. At night the seasons shuffle

their greasy playing cards, stars
roll fuzzy dice in sky, and our fathers wear their second jobs
like sacks of dwarfs who whistle
on their backs. *I love you*

our mothers will say to them
one last time before they die, and our
fathers will just drive, grunt, nod, while

a hot-white car-lot light searches
the local sky for life.

Crow's Feet

The crows are larger than you, and they
have voices that sew stitches
and zippers across the sky, though
no one cries all day when they die. The sleepy

gazes of the fountain's Sirens stretch
a mucused web across the lawn, while

the milkweed pods just nod
at one another, silver
and dumb. Soon enough their careful faces
will split their seams and spill

a bleating issue of ghost-hair
into a sedated breeze, and

still the crows that balance the wall
to which the whole coincidence
and mystery has been fused
all along — those

crows just chat on blandly
all day about your death, your
age, how much you've managed to change (as if

overnight). Oh

overnight there's either dancing
and drinking in infinity, or grief
and the crows come orange-stamping at
your eyes to cool their tired wire feet

in tears, which turn
to wet cement while you sleep.

Aqua

The cool kiss of a fetus, it
hasn't any bones
and it can only say, Take
this ocean, take this air, take
the motel pool with its soft hair. What's

aqua in this world
of simple browns and grays, won't
survive for long, I know, but I've

seen the one I lost, and now it rides
a white moth in a fabricated sky *too*
close to the light, but I'm

not its mother anymore, although
the lust that made it still
comes clumsy, and it goes, like
a drunken friend who's made

ruin of the house a hundred times, and
still comes knocking with his fists
of cold water and hope. *Here's*

the rain you ordered, Room
Service says, *and*
the artificial fog, the luke-
warm water, and the bathing suits. The lips

of the boy in the pool's deep end
have turned blood-blue, though
he's feverish and large, and his mother
can barely hold him
up above the water

and his father has a bald spot like a saucer
of milk left overnight
for a jet-black cat
by the back porch door. Their

hands lift the child between them together
into chlorinated air, water
parting around their boy
like a tender eye, while

the boy sputters out, laughing
and alive. The way
a cervix is a sea-thing, too, whether
you notice or not. It

shrinks and blooms when the fetus
reaches out toward it, swimming
for the light. Later

his mother will sit
in a lounge chair next to mine, *He's
only got a month or less to live,*
she'll say, *and he wanted to spend it*

at the Holiday Inn. I see then

how this pool-blue is illusional
and *made*, and back

in the cool dark mildew of our room, I'll
grow terribly afraid. I'll
dream the boy is mine, and he's
slipping quickly through a plastic tube.
Light

weaves above him
like a radiant ballet, and I'll

wake to a woman's voice as it
rises and falls above me
as if from far away — a warm
palate pulsing diphthongs, like

comfort's soft wave
on a small safe lake: They say

this color in a dream
could easily mean Life — but I'm

relieved to find it's only
the butcher who's been going
door-to-door again tonight, knocking
and knocking in his

old suit of red and white.

TEN

from *Wild Brides*

...as if it had never been.

The Cyclone

When I am sixteen I think
I'm falling in love with a boy
who's learning to play the electric guitar.
Hour after hour
passes by in his basement
in the blur of noise he is doing.
I sit on an old couch
and stare at him
until I hear only
a flutter of motion around my head
like a hot, churning bath.
For a moment he stops
and my empty head howls
the lull of a train
racing around and around me
until I finally drop dazed
out of a windstorm, many years
ahead of myself. The world
is Technicolor and turning
and suddenly I'm
the mother of the boy who is learning
to play the electric guitar. It's beautiful, summer, Saturday outside
and he's been down there all day with a girl.
The strain of it, the endless crescendo,
the bedlam of music and motion
lifts the house
into air, explodes
the sonic boom of breaking
the barriers of sound,
the upward locomotion
of making dinner, making love, waking up
every day after day after day, the rumbling
of a platform in the past

where I am sixteen
and waiting for a train
while down the street
an old, deaf woman
is planting cabbage behind a shed.

The Driver's Lullaby

for Cary, who slept at the wheel

You drive until you pass the place
the sun sets   until you pass the place
the gypsy moths catch fire
and our souls store up like rain

in old cans   and the blue plums turn
to macadam   and the asphalt
blushes roses   where
the last light makes and snuffs itself.

It's a long drive   flagstone, cobblestone
and the body has its limits. We
are all just weak as flesh in the end
and sleep rouses us   billows us

like bedsheets in the wind   bedsheets
your mother hung in summer.
When you see this again
it is with no sound but cicada hum

or the static rattle of the past:
a burst of cardinal in the lilacs
startles you   and the sky
above you is so blinding

it requires you to be music   and you
are only the size of your own arm
in your crib. When your young mother
turns to you   she's holding

fatigue out in her arms   and it's
only a scarf of air   but then

the field turns to black
and barbed wire   and for a moment you

see yourself   in a cow's white eye
driving to sulfur and tin and air
and the hole in the earth where
the soul collects itself. While

up ahead   in this night's small town
a barber pole whirls eternal stripes
through the dark. And you
drive past that, too.

Hymn from the House of Trouble

So go now my love before you're gone.
Before you're older, sadder, sicker,
gone, though I'll still be
awake and waiting.
I have nowhere else
I want to go.

To go to the door of the House of Trouble
and decide I want to stay
even when they tell me,
There will be three nights of pleasure followed
by thirty years' bad luck.
I say, Fine. Let me sleep with that one,
the one the others are afraid of,
the one with the evil twin.

The evil twin with a bottle
who pins my hands behind my back,
whose name is the name of a saint,
a drunken fair-haired angel from hell
passed out all night like a child in my arms.

There are hymns all night in the House of Trouble,
sacred snapshots of the dead,
sobbing and giggling among the girls,
hysterical, empty cups in the sink.

And all the men are drinkers,
slow drinkers drinking until
they only look like men I love,
until I only love the way they look.

The way he looks, the way he looks.
And the smell of his shirts.

And when his hands, and when his hands.
I'm tangled to death in my own sheets,
gasping and snagged like a trout.

See all these are snapshots of you
looking green-eyed at the beach.
All these snapshots are you before
the bottle in your hand is empty
and all your buddies are maudlin or brawling,
all of you still for a second smiling
like beautiful monsters clapping each other,
sequined and rising from the great, green lake.

So leave my love because I've become a believer.
And I believe in another God, another life,
a better, harder, longer life to come
and I'll come back and back to this place I am

and when I do
it will be with you,
it will be you again.

Timespan

It's no wider than the span of my arms.
As the camera pans farther   and farther
from me, this becomes smaller
and smaller   and smaller

until   I'm back in my mother's body, I'm
the coldness at the center
of that scalding body, I'm no more
than a chip of ice in her burning girlhood.

She is dressed in white for Scarlet Fever
and the doctors expect her to die, her blood
is seawater infused with fire   and I
am oblivion curled away in a cave

of red-hot flowers. Perhaps God
would like to spade over my grave   but
it's winter, the cold ceramic
of the washbowl burns her cheek

and cold-blooded birds flash wings as white
as His beard by her window. It starts
to snow   snow   and snow until
if the snow were any deeper, it would be the sky.

A train screeches its brakes out there
where my grandmother is standing
in boots and her camel's hair coat, watching
her only child die. This

is as close as they'll let her get. It falls
on all of us there, the metal
ringing of train wheels, fresh
blood on those tracks   and timespan

spirals to the deeper circles
of our hells. My mother smolders
and my grandmother shakes the snow
like ashes from her hair, white

hospital paint peels around the windows.
So   what's a miracle? I
lurch out of the frozen ground then   full-
bloomed and red as a poison rose

and my mother turns to the steamy window
and smiles   at her own mother, who can see
the red strings of shredded flesh
between her daughter's gleaming teeth.

The Sorceress and the Wife

She decided she had to have
her neighbor's husband
one summer in the suburb:
in the green
energy of desire, in the heat
lightning of lust.

I asked my friend his wife, Didn't
you ever suspect?

She said, What would I have supposed?
She was our neighbor, our friend, our widow next door.
Black butterflies drifted, amiably,
between our lawns.
Elms lined up like soldiers down the street.
How would I have known
in the ordinary evening, the polite
string quartet of summer, that
a sorceress fell in love with my husband?

In the orderly evening, in the beautiful
backyard with a beer, he
was an angel asleep in a lawn chair,
one eye closed.

I asked my friend his wife, Weren't
you ever, even, suspicious?
No, she told me, how
could I have known
that my life was a dream I could wake up from?

A moss-green dream, peacock
green, aquamarine, and fading.

He was dozing by the sprinkler, his chest
as cool as the skin of a pear and shirtless.

I asked, Wasn't there ever a sign? She tried
to remember, but there was only
the one early summer evening
a truck of pigs passed the house
on detour off the freeway, reeking
in the heat, squealing — peach-
and silken-fleshed
as a truck of rotten children.

He stretched and sipped from the beer. The
top button of his Bermudas came undone.

Bells of Ice

Nothing's as perfect as gravity.
Even the water would try
to keep us from drowning.
But gravity wants
to bring back winter. Tuesday's

as cold as December
in the middle of summer, and
every hour they turn her
to keep the skin from fraying.
The lake swallows the beach.

Even the water would try, but
gravity turns our existence against us,
turns the weight of being alive
into a burden
of bedsores and trying to die.

A nurse has come to turn her, turn
her, tumble her
out of her life.

She is plummeting into the tunnel. She
is whirling into the tunnel.
And I can feel the wind, can imagine
the beach today, gasping
in the chill.

I try to hold a snapshot up
for her to see. My dead grandfather's arm
is around her. They
clink glasses some summer.
Cold beautiful bells of ice. Father
and daughter, a picnic

table, and a beach.
The lime-gray glasses raised —
A toast!

To anything!
Arbitrary,
our lives, so

what is the sense in staying?

The tunnel takes
our memories, too, tortures us later
with our own old snapshots,
our little recollections

of last kisses before deaths.
The tacky statues

we remember
one another with.

All that love and that long stretch of beach
are gone, and pitiful, and useless to recall.

We are falling
one by one into its face. The eye
of the tunnel glitters, gaudy
and mocking, just

to show us our folly, just
to empty us for the journey.

Solomon Grundy

Born on Monday to mucus and blood
and the arms of a teenage mother
slippery with dread, under a moon that crept
with mushrooms in the dark
while the bloodsuckers sucked and clung
to the dead. The world
is as watery as a womb, he thought,
gurgling and murky with tears.

Baptized on Tuesday with water and weeping
on a day so damp the frogs were dripping
in ecstasy out of the trees
and the priest was singing, "I exorcise thee,"
and the warm wet diaper chilled
to the burning and blazing of sleet
and the Mary of Misery with her bare white feet
pierced his bladder with her plaster stare
and Solomon Grundy shivered and screamed.

Married on Wednesday for fairer or fouler
because the milk was warm in her veins
and the meat was sweet on her limbs
and the church bells shrieked in the steeples
and the housefly slept in the feces.
And where they met he was bathed
by the smooth white tongues of their sheets.
There was peace for a while and love and she said,
We have gone together now to a place
from which there is no return.
His pleasure uncurled in her like the mercy of sperm.

Took ill on Thursday in the summer shade
of a fever tree, and the priest screamed,
"I exorcise thee!" and the nurse burst in

with her purse full of pills
and a lock of his hair, and spittle
and toads. They bandaged him,
x-rayed him, amputated all
his watery toes, and never gave up hope until
the last coin rolled from his pocket, and still
on Friday he was ill.

Solomon Grundy got worse on Friday
and the sun washed away in the rain
and a nun flapped past in the inky wind.
His wife gave up and went home
where she slid right down into the oily mud
slick with the tongue of the neighbor's son.
And Solomon Grundy, toeless and blind,
listened to soap operas all afternoon, and he cried.

On Saturday Solomon Grundy died
and the priest buzzed around his corpse like a fly
and his mother picked maggots out of his eye
and his wife wiped the flower dry that wept
for another between her thighs.
And the slugs and the nothing clung and sucked.

Embalmed and gutted and buried on Sunday,
and that is the end of Solomon Grundy.

Woman Kills Sweetheart with Bowling Ball

The moon is loose in the gutter tonight
and it rolls without kisses
or handprints between us   Its mouth
is an O of surprise

O   Tonight the phantasma of love
climbs the stairs while we sleep   She
sags with exhaustion and booze
and pills   while her skin hangs heavy
and empty as hate
She floats so slow she floats
as if she is swimming through blood

> *Shhh   Shhh*   the lights are out
> and the little suspicion
> sleeps and dreams
> and whimpers in its crib
> Its tongue is ugly and blue

She climbs   She climbs
in silence and fury   spinning groggy
in darkness and wind   Look
her left hand bears for you sweetly
a gift of lightning
and lilies to please you   Though

O   tonight
in her right hand she   she
has invented gravity

To Whom It May Concern

During the winter   I stayed indoors
and rattled the cups   brained
the tomatoes and canned them   until
the teapot shrieked and the tea
turned brackish and   smelled like bile
and the shoe tree bloomed in the closet   Then
I sent a simple note:

Please   please   marry me   The daisies
on the curtains are eggish
and bleed   and the pork
reeks on the plate   and I have become a girl
huge and dreadful with love
like a mushroom cloud floating luminous over the lake

Lift me out of this house
as you might lift a child
trapped in the scraps of a car   The edges of this house
are razor sharp
and the collision here has left several dead

I tell you   I
will be limp and simple with pain —

the bed for sex and the fork for food

Please   marry me   lift me
out of this house
where my father takes my tongue
like a lover   where the family portrait
wails on the wall
where I've danced all winter
among the rubble   clumsy
and pointless on a rag rug

for the stove   obscene in his gaping
for the toaster's terrible grin

I tell you   I'll be
a guileless wife   rustic
and homely as a farmhouse in snow

Rosebush

I have dug up my grandfather   accidentally
while planting the rosebush behind the shed

His long-buried hair is as gentle and white
as a web, and the spider is silver
and spinning it   spinning it
as he rises and says to me: Now

I don't have much time to explain, my dear
so you'll have to make all the arrangements
yourself   Be sure to prepare a place
for each of us there

My grandfather speaks to me kindly from death
and the words are so bright they fly
around his head like a shower
of dazzling birds   and I am relieved to see
that the simple grave
could press all that pain
into light like stars in my own backyard   where

someday my children can chip at that bitterness
with chisels and picks
and shine it and hold it
up to the sun   to see the pain plainly in death
as I could never see it in life   *Children:*

This is the place where your
great-grandfather turned to glass   He
was a man who wept bits of glitter
who was never without a drink in his life
and who liked to drink his torment raw

He was a kind man who hated children
but loved a victim   and knew
all of the tenderest places to grope
and the wounded for miles knew him
and called him by name

But look   his suffering has turned
to a dust of sparks so fine it startles the eye

The grave must finally suit him
The grave must please him greatly

He says to me: *Now*
Be sure there is plenty for everyone there
and don't be afraid   we can be home by Monday
and no one will know we were gone

I'm delirious with joy   as a feverish child
and I see that he is the source of all music

of all the music my life has made   from him
a blinding choir shines
and I finally cry   on my knees
in the dirt   with an armful of thorns   and I
am ready to leave with him   anywhere   ready
to take every one of them with me   But when

the day
comes (and it finally does)

I am not so sure   I am not so sure
I am ready to go

I see you will live an ordinary life, perhaps
have children, perhaps marry
a kind but un-
remarkable man. There
is a simple journey that waits for you
(Niagara Falls? Yellowstone Park?). Go
on it. Make
the decisions you have to make: paint
the upstairs bathroom blue, move
to Wisconsin. It doesn't matter.
But here, here in this crease, this crease
like a scar at your thumb — here
I see something more.
The drapes in this room will be red
and torn. Close them. Let him
show you slowly to the bed. No
you'll say, it's daylight
and my simple husband trusts me.
Trust me — this
is your moment — the one
you'll remember (the hot breath
of the August breeze, the sun
white in the sky, the trickle of sweat
on his neck: it will turn to salt on your tongue).
This one you've held
and will hold all your life
though it cuts a bit at your thumb
like a single sliver of glass that glints
from a quarry of slate. You
will die someday, of course, slowly
not young, not old. And before you're forgotten
the neighbors will speak of you fondly.
Now   close your hand tight
on this secret. Die

with this secret but no regrets. Remember
this is how the small survive, the way
the small have always survived.

Godmother's Advice

Sweetheart, the world
and everything in it
and the backward spinning forward
while the chips fall and the blue fruit
consumes us: All

will be later and nothing, too,
where the branches blacken the trees
like winter and winter then suddenly spring:
The men will be angry, and
the bloodclots, and
the gallstones

but don't cry: Listen
to the hum and the drum for omens —
for everything happens when we
are just about to relax, and the pigs
are snoring swinely in their pails:

Try to stay alive until you die.
Some night you will find yourself
singing in your car
on a street too far from where you live
and the radio on, and your eyes are tired:

Suddenly the street is a river of ice
and you are spinning in both lanes and learning
these laws of physics:
All the trees grow in the path of the wind
for a reason, and a billiard ball will roll

at the exact speed of the ball
that hits it from behind: The click

and spin of balls in the dark
and a truck whirls to you
and the windshield will kiss you

and laughter, and clapping. Remember:
The world is vulgar and everything in it:
The sweet of the melon
and the meat-pie steam of being alive.
You will be crying

for more of that: The clock
will rant in the waiting room
while the pallbearer stumbles in his shoes
and you will be stunned
and stillborn into the street.

ELEVEN

New Poems

Now... a wall, wondrously high...

House to House

Poems, like doctors. Like
postmen, ordeals. Like

the sun setting onto the slate, making
an artistic catastrophe out
of the end of an ordinary day.
Oooh, we say, as the violence
sinks into space, mouth agape.

Gods, like sobs in prayers — so
many of us calling out at once
we have to learn to share. Like

the moths of the suburbs going
from porch to porch
in jilted swarms.
Remember how

every summer night
as the lights went out
they made their rounds, wearing
their tattered hospital gowns?

Spies

There may be hundreds of white birds that aren't called
doves. But
it's too late to wake my husband, and
I'm too tired to look it up. So

tonight, to me, they're all called
doves, doves, doves. And someone's

stitched my soul to one, or
so it seems to me because

tonight, I'm riding her white wing as she
carries the coded message of my mortality
with her across the Atlantic, the Pacific, the Gulf
of Mexico — completely free
of our two bodies, despite
the mastectomies, the
reconstructive surgeries…

Or, could she be, instead, that *other* dove? The one we've all

seen dusted, and deloused, and perched on a plastic branch
behind glass, permanently smudged

with children's fingerprints at the Natural History Museum?

They stare, those children, at her. And the men, they
stare as well, as they stroll
with their younger wives, their lovers, the lovers of their wives.

Her breast, no longer white. Her soul?

Oh, God — what if it's *her* soul that has been stitched to *mine?*

And if — ?

Well, if it is — then this would be her white, and this
my wing —

And, if it is — well, if it is, how
quiet the humans' house must seem to her tonight, as I —

as *we* —

move about it
turning off the lights. Tiptoeing. Holding our breath:

How quiet this place, this night. How full of spies.

Innocence

The beautiful girl who stripped off her clothes
at the party by the pond, to dive.

And all the boys who turned around to watch. *Oh
my God.* And there she goes. While the rest of us

stood around the fire, also girls, in our down coats.
Pointless. Not even close

to naked, and not even able to wish her drowned
because a tragedy would only make a thing like her

more beautiful, being tragic, as everybody knows.
And now — look at these young things on the Internet,

who just lie down. Or so it seems: simplicity. Their
immortality, already done, long before it's

even begun. They're like trees with their branches
in a forest, thrashing around

in a storm, but the storm's long over.
There's always that expression, as in the eyes

of the dog after knocking its master's plate to the floor.
Shame nudging a little gate open, accidentally, to a path

back into innocence, which is always waiting. This
way: to this leafy, secret, personal place in the brain.

Its shade is reserved for all of us, and for the many
decisions we made, or never made, or decided

to decide we'd never made. Having managed, somehow,
after all these years to trade our places:

the naked one, the others. You
in your down coat. You, naked.

All of us wishing we'd simply been watching
from a distance, wearing tiny feathers, hating.

Instead of naked, swimming. But aren't
we innocent, all of us, after all this time?

No one here is to blame: surely, all these things
we did and didn't do are now the same.

The Names of the Trees

I passed this place long ago
when a man lived here with his
four daughters, peacefully, it seemed.

Those daughters took turns washing
dishes, doing laundry. Frothy pearls and
feathers in a sink. Soft

socks, warm towels, folded, clean, in
closets, drawers, and baskets, and
on shelves. To me

this was astonishing. The laundry
done by daughters! No
mother in the house at all! A weeping

willow grew in their back-
yard, but it was not a symbol then.
It could not have been

because this was the only tree
I knew the name of yet — unless it was a tree
that bore familiar fruit. Like

an apple tree, a mulberry. This
willow's branches did not seem to be
branches at all to me, but

ribbons dangling loosely, tangling
girlishly. If there was any weeping, it
was inaudible to me. (Was

I supposed to *see* it?) One
of the daughters was only
a year ahead of me, and she

invited me (once only) over
to play House with me. When
I confessed I wasn't sure what playing

House might mean, this girl said
she'd teach me.
She was Mother for this reason.

I was the family dog. She
told me to eat Fruit Loops
from a bowl on the kitchen floor

while on my hands and knees. We
laughed when I couldn't do it. But when
I was Mother, she

couldn't do it either:
That there was laughter!
A blue tablecloth.

Salt and pepper shakers shaped
like hands, which, put
together, appeared to pray. When

I was thirsty, another daughter poured
a cup of water for me, pouring
water with such confidence it

seemed to me that she
might have poured the first water
from the first tap. When, out

of curiosity, I went
into their bathroom and pretended to pee
I witnessed toilet paper printed with

forget-me-nots, along with a little dish
that held a piece of pink soap in it.
And, when, after this, I couldn't sleep

for three nights in a row, my
mother finally gave up
trying to comfort me.

The Face

The only other patient here today —
A blonde I saw ten years ago, gone gray.
And why would I recall this woman's face
When so much else I've seen has slipped away?

A total stranger really. Dissolving wall
Between my memory and her and all
The tin toys wound too tight, the funerals —
While she's been locked inside me. I'm a vault!

A dresser drawer! Silk underthings, white lies —
A woman's face. A decade passing while
I tried to hail a cab that just sped by —
And she was in it, staring out, free ride

In someone else's memory. She smiled
And disappeared, it seemed. Married well,
I'm sure. And tended roses. Wrote her novels.
At the center of her wedding cake, a bell

Made out of even sweeter cake. I've tasted
Bells myself. In vivid rooms, I've waited
As jellied fruit was passed around, vows taken.
What money buys. What beauty, as it fades —

"I know you," if I knew her, I would say.
But what is she to me now anyway?
A blonde I saw ten years ago, gone gray —
The other patient waiting here today.

The pages of my magazine are thin.
The music of a crow has been piped in.
Nurse, overweight. The doctor's late again.
I find my iPhone in my purse, and then —

Her bald child (a girl, perhaps eleven)
Is wheeled into the room to rest her head
Between her mother's broken heart and broken

Wing. Broken and forgotten, everything.

Rockefeller Plaza

How, in eighth grade, we
got philosophy
and began to discuss what it might mean
if I were simply imagining
you imagining me.

But we each assumed the other one
was the invented one. Unless
you truly did not exist, and so
you simply humored me.

I sure hope not:

To think I could be alone here, not
even on a darkling plain: Just me

concocting armies, far-off wars. All these
newspaper accounts of my
atrocities, not

to mention all, with my own eyes, I've
believed I've seen:

Hawk on a golf course, and
that rabbit seeming to sing.

My mother pleading with me
not to let the nurses eat her.
Please, please…

How could I allow such things
even in a memory
if it's all just me?

But then, of course, I think:

This would also mean that it was I
who created a parent's love for a child!

And who would it have been
who placed and labeled in that museum
all those ancient trinkets in
that glass case but me? And

for tinfoil and for cherries, you'd
also have me to thank, it seems.

And even for the thousands of you
gathered here tonight
because of me —

each with your own face, and name, and
waiting very patiently
for my municipality
to light your Christmas tree.

Yes —
all your voices, all this wonderment
expressed in one massive
human yawn, an

emotional cloud issuing
from all of us at once

as its lights snap on.

How good it was of you to be
here to see it, too, with me.
Not to be alone, not to witness
such a thing without
the rest of you. All

of you — my beloveds, my dearest
strangers, who so generously
shared your awe with me. Or

so I let myself believe.

Champagne

A cold wind, later, but no rain.
A bus breathing heavily at the station.
Beggars at the gate, and the moon
like one bright horn of a white
cow up there in space. But

really, must I think about all of this
a second time in this short life?

This crescent moon, like a bit
of ancient punctuation. This

pause in the transience of all things.

Up there, Ishtar in the ship
of life she's sailing. Has

she ripped open again
that sack of grain?
Spilled it all over the place?
Bubbles rising to the surface, breaking.

They've set down our glasses of champagne
beside our sharpened blades.
A joke is made.
But, really, must

I hear this joke again?

Must I watch the spluttering
light of this specific flame? Must

I consider forever the permanent
transience of all things:

The bus, breathing at the station.
The beggars at the gate.
The girl I was.
Both pregnant and chaste.
The cold wind, that crescent moon.
No rain.

What difference
can it possibly make, that
pain, now that not a single
anguished cry of it remains?

So, really, must I grieve it all again?
And why tonight

of all the nights, and just
as I'm about to raise, with
the blissful others, my

glass to the silvery, liquid
chandelier above us?

Ubi sunt

"20 Basic Tech Things Old People Just Don't Understand,"
Cosmopolitan magazine

There it goes, her bathrobe
in the talons of a hawk. It goes, and so she
steps out naked
in her naked shame — a sagging, scarred, and all-gray thing.

And then the rest of her, around her ankles, it
drops down. Over. It's
all gone. While

the children, those Immortals, have left her here alone.
Their Carnival Cruises. Those titanic ships. Drunk

on their ambrosias. Laughing, snorting, eating little
plates of sausages, green peas, singing karaoke, while

not even. Not even her feet. (As if on loan, these feet, from
some feral, feline, tailed and green-eyed beast.) And

the path she must have crossed with those, not
knowing that she'd crossed it. While

also being *streaming* feet. Forget

the quantum physics of all this, and that
physicist. Who is this? The one
with that disease. She

remembers, instead, Lou Gehrig (or
"Buster" they called him, or "The Iron Horse" before —).

Lou Gehrig on a cruise ship, too. His wife
with him, and his best friend, Babe Ruth, and
Babe Ruth's girlfriend. And

health, and youth, and dancing girls. Photographers
and seagulls. Calm seas. Tuxedos. Champagne —

And Lou Gehrig, All-Star champion (seven times).
And Lou Gehrig, American League Most Valuable Player (twice).
His .340 batting average. His .632 slugging average. His
493 home runs. Elected

in 1939 to the Baseball Hall of Fame. 1,995 RBI. And then

one day, on board that ship, Lou
Gehrig could not find his wife. He

searched, and called her name
for an hour or so before he panicked, found
the captain, and

an alarm went up (of course, as
such alarms must be sent up) — the ship's horn, and every

passenger took up the cry. It was
a wild hunt for Lou Gehrig's wife, until

the worst of all worst things had finally to be
considered, as eventually these worst things must
always be: that Mrs. Gehrig had

slipped on the deck, perhaps, or she'd
leapt to her own death, so that

now she was down there, drifting and drifting to the bottom
of that wide, cold, unfathomably deep, cold sea. But then —

But then a little later, a maid with a master key found
Lou Gehrig's wife in
Babe Ruth's cabin
in Babe Ruth's bed —

where now their naked radiance was
sweet and smoothly there on fire, or
so the maid with the master key said.

And not long after that (how fast it passes, how
without warning) the sound, perhaps, that
Lou Gehrig might have heard before
his death — the paralysis of such an ocean's depths.

Or his wife with his best friend. The children

glowing on their little screens, sending photos of the sea
snapped by their little, unholy machines. Saying, "See

us. See us smiling. Happily. Ruthlessly. Posing ourselves
in front the world's few, last, sacred, ancient things. We've

turned our backs to them — these
shrines and paintings and cathedrals, the likes
of which will not, perhaps, ever be

created on Earth again — so
that you might see, instead, our faces here in front of them."

But, truly, *never again?*

No, no, sweet old lady bathing. We are no different
from those who came before us. No

different from those, who
in their greatness — ?

Where now?

On the Properties of Summer

The rosebush foams, but not the flag (no
breeze at all) exhausted on its pole — as if
the battle had been lost, or
the thinker's lost the thought, or
the pastor's head were bowed as he
read, into a hole, a psalm.

Some bees, abuzz, seem
to drown together in the pond. Crazy
zigzag dance across the black. "Could

our bus driver be drunk?" an elderly
woman asks an elderly man. But then

the diner, the others with their canes
behind those two, and the refrigerated
carousel with the cakes. The yawn

of the waitress, long day, and some-

one points out the flattened grass back
there behind it all, the place
where the children roll
in the park on Saturdays, and the way

the sun across the street appears to cling
like a cat
to the teenage lawn boy's naked back.

Pandora's Mouth

Who was told to keep it shut
but who opened it anyway, to sing
the secrets of the boy she loved — and then
instead of a song, a fountain of troubles poured
out, bubbled up. Doubled over in the parking lot
as pink froth, as the waters of a life mixed in with a bit
of her heart's blood, as he called out from his
hell again & again, "I just asked you to keep
your mouth shut. Why couldn't
you just keep it shut?"

In the Meantime

Today I saw one hatch, that
damp surprise inside the incubator at
Family Farm & Feed, and

I recognized, instantly, my
old epiphany, the one that once arrived to me in
the back of a classroom to which I'd been banished
for snipping the sleeve of my own sweater
with a pair of rounded scissors I'd been given

to cut a donkey's tail
for a game I was to play.

How could you do that, Laura? Your
poor mother knitted that sweater for you…

The rest of that day's lessons, and that game, went
on and on without me. My
friends' backs turned to me. And

it was then I understood how they were made
of light, each one of them, entirely, and that
for some reason, I, a solidity, had
found myself among them
in this world I'd never
been meant to see
let alone to be in.

An ancient mistake had been made, it seemed, but
recently, and I'd arrived
just in time to be its victim, as
well as its beneficiary. For

I had been intended for some other, darker place.
Some planet without a warm gold star lolling
around above it. The others

knew perfectly well
what it was, what
it was for, and how it had gotten there.
I watched them draw its circles and spikes
with yellow crayons. Experts, every
one of them. But they

weren't about to explain it, knowing
that it wasn't there for me. But

there I was among them anyway.
Nothing anyone could do about it. In

the meantime, from back there, I
could study, very carefully, their ways

and whatever they wanted to hear
was what I wanted to say.

After the funeral in the basement of the church, always
the feast. Always the elderly aunt complaining
about the carrot salad. (Far too sweet.) And someone
accidentally tossed the guestbook into the trash. Now
how is the dead one supposed to know who skipped
the service, stayed home to watch the Super Bowl instead?

Baked beans. Cold cement. Cinder block. A framed
print of the Last Supper faded above the coffee urn.
The coffee, dripping onto a saucer, scorched. A dog
barks from a car in the parking lot. A cart's wooden
wheels clatter across a wooden bridge. The peasants
returning to the fields. The king and queen asleep.

And the cows stop ruminating for a minute to listen.

The thick water of certain liquors. The hidden bits
of our bodies — silent, rubied, slimed. Like
ovaries, or tonsils, like
all things pried from their shells, held up to the light.

Yes: this phlegmy knot. I wanted to tell you something
before you died, but swallowed it accidentally, like an eye.

Delirium

Only for twenty minutes or so, but —

I once found myself at delirium's core, where

the delirious seeds were
given to me, so that I emerged with my fist closed
tightly around these.

Oh, I thought, they'll be
my favorite slaves, my little demons, my trivial
angels, my drunken bridesmaids — or

my unborn baby's playmates on a summer's day.

And, after thinking that, I
watched as the dead one
chased the others to the edge
of everything, and then
all of it faded away.

You were loved, it seems, if such a thing
can be judged by the volume of the weeping.

Nice suit. A fine day for a funeral. Not

too hot, a few blue clouds, your wife like a trail
through apple trees in bloom
on the way to the picnic tables.

It's spring, too, so there's
spring's perfume
of promise & rot.
And your son looks just like you. Even

from where I sit in this back pew, I can see
that this could very well be
what you might have wanted, had
you been able to imagine
such a thing as your own funeral — back

then at one of those four bad
high school dances you took me to.

Not exactly *that*, but not its opposite, either. There

could be a local band in this place, too.
"Smoke on the Water"
throbbing against the roof. Even
"Hey Jude" so loud, remember?
So loud we stuffed our ears with toilet paper just
so we could stand to stand outside the gym and scream
affectionate things to one another. Oh

how our pores opened, poured
forth our hormones, and our
veins, tangled, pulsed
with blood, while

beneath our arms and between our legs, those
curled black hairs
sprouted there, while all of this
was smothered under
the most ridiculous clothes we'd ever wear —

scratchy, tight, and sad. But you

never failed to insist that I
was the most beautiful girl in every room in what-
ever desperate dress I'd finally persuaded
my mother at the mall to let me choose, and

I might have believed you, too, until
I saw myself in a mirror, wearing

polyester, sweating mascara.

And the hunger, and the thirst. Tantalus
up to his neck in
a particular type of Midwestern pollution —

sludge and dung and tarnished spoons. The

popcorn too salty, the pop too warm, and in

that special hell in which
the dancers danced — electrocuted, maniacked — it was
eternally too dark and hot, while out
here with the other standers (how
you hated to dance!) too bright, too bright, and always

the double doors to the parking lot were propped
open to a snowstorm, so you
put your blazer
over my bare shoulders, and

trembled in your shirtsleeves
in the cold. But

we were young, and pretty much untouched, and

happy enough.
Or at least I was. And there's

some comfort in that now — a couple

hours before they put you in the ground (a last
hurrah for which I will not hang around) — this

knowledge that, back when
we did not know what sensual
pleasure was, or what

we were missing, we were not

suffering then, so

you must not suffer now, again, my love.

March

It's the murderer who got away with it, sitting
on a park bench, thinking about snow

and how it's over. Little flower-faces peeking
out of dirt to shriek *Hello!*

While mothers wheel babies by, absurdly
bright. Businessmen in amber. And the light

on steeples served up in cones of white. But—
something here is also not quite right. Old

lady in a little girl's bonnet. Ugly dog with
a child's smile. Always, it seems, in

spring you'll find someone with regrets
she's allowed herself to forget:

Eye at the keyhole. Milk in the saucepan, and
that strange kiss that went on and on and on.

Envelope Addressed to Me with Your Return Address

The street we used to live on bore the name
of a man who had to be told
one day by a stranger, "Sir, sit down," and then, "It

seems your son has fallen from a train."

And our town was named for the place
from which our founding fathers were
forced to flee one bloody day. They

managed to stuff their traveling trunks with
all the shame they could carry, and when
they got here with it they said, "Let's

forget all that, start over here, but
keep the name."

And the wolf that mated
with the mother of the neighbor's dog —
in that shadow of the valley of the shadows
was never seen again. Now, Bailey
howls some nights exactly like
a bad memory, without a name —

one I also
managed to repress
until this businesslike envelope arrives one day —
sealed, it seems, with the very tongue that once
so lovingly uttered a pet name I grew to hate.

And your return address.
And *your* name:

The darkest night of my life
masquerading for decades as a name.

The Hunt

Once, I sat down in a forest and forced myself to recall the last conversation we ever had.

Once, I sat down in that vast grove, haunted with its gentle, mischievous creatures. At the end of every path, a magical cat. A small funny monkey called Sprite. An owl that could twist its head around and around on its neck just for my delight.

But then the fog rolled over it all. I saw caves and hollow trees stuffed with stolen altarpieces. I'd invented it, I realized. It was my net of nerves tossed desperately over a cloud of moths. It was a long parade of technocrats and monks. I watched them shuffle in chains toward me, emerging (hymnals, candlesticks) down the forest's path out of my sad past.

Oh, yes, a herd of reindeer. Lovely beasts. Blinking, they were blinking. *It will bloom just as wildly in your garden this summer as it will bloom next year on your grave.*

All these noble impulses and sacred memories in the same place as that stupid country song with its maddening refrain. To lie to oneself — it is nothingness added to more of itself.

Praying Mantis in My Husband's Salad

Once, he found one
among the lettuce leaves and
cabbage shreds a former
girlfriend had

arranged on a plate for him. If

it was still alive, I can't
remember what my husband said that
he and the girlfriend did with it. But
so it is, this

remembrance of the stories of the days of love
with another love of the one you love. She had

blue eyes. He told me that. And
long black hair. She
may or may not have worn glasses. If

she did she would have looked like a scholar in them, and
then the whole sexy scholar thing when she took them off
to lie down beside him on the bed. This

was long before I met him. So
why should I be jealous, or even sad? Even

stranger is
how can I remember it?
And remember it so well?

But I can — having
seen some praying mantises myself.
Their switchblade limbs. The precision
of their folding insectness.

And their Martian faces, of course, with
such innocent expressions.
But all-knowing.
And all business.
And the lettuce-green of them. This

bitch, I looked her up
on the Internet. She's
still alive, in California, where she teaches something
pointless, like linguistics. But

here's the thing: He's never, my
husband, been
a salad-eater. Was he then? Was

the praying mantis he found once in his lettuce
the reason he has eaten
no salad since I met him?

Or was he just in love? Was

he trying to please this salad-tossing girlfriend
from the past, who
offered up to him the last pale-green thing
he'd ever eat again?

Maybe they were brown, her eyes.
Now, I can't remember that, but I'd

bet you any amount of money that her legs were
long, and that she shaved them in his bathtub
with his razor. Her

neck, elegant as a swan's, blah-blah.
But then, imagine

it, their surprise, and just
try not to laugh out loud:

My tiny, triangular head, swiveling
from side to side. My
dead expression, while

my arms (sharpened swords, in fact — for I've
been seen to slice and eat a hummingbird
on National Geographic) seemed

folded up in supplication, or in praise, or in
solemn meditation, just

as they were spreading out their napkins
on their laps, and
raising, perhaps, their glasses in a toast
to the meal she'd made for him, and which
they were about to share, beginning

with that salad, and
also ending there.

Bored Girl Spits into an Abyss

There were plenty of decades during which
I worried a lot about what love was. But

it was never a *what* that I wondered.
Or a *know* I believed I could get.
No. It was more like the wall they'd leave behind
after they knocked the cathedral down.
I supposed. Something symbolic.
Or an illusion. The way

some summer nights when I was a child
it seemed the air, darkening, grew so excited
it turned to fireflies. But, of course, that

wasn't it. These
were completely separate events.
The confusion
of a kid.
So maybe
that was it, I thought.
And I thought a lot about it.
Swimming along like a drop

of rain in a flood: All wrong
about what and where I was.
And love —

It was, as it turns out, that
bored teenage girl who'd leaned
too far over the railing
to spit into the abyss.

"For God's sake!"
I screamed at her, and she

gave me the finger
when she turned around, and said, "Fuck!
You almost made me fall, you bitch!"

Yes. That was it. It was that, which

was also our toddler, happily howling when
we used to swing him in the space
between ourselves
by his fat little hands. Appearing

to surrender him
while holding on. Like —

Well, like that popular song.
Or like nothing. Like

nothing else becoming more
of itself, which was

a thrill and a vow
at once, and how

obvious, I realized, when
she turned around, all
pissed off, it had
been all along.

Daysleep

Remember sleep, in May, in the afternoon, like
a girl's bright feet slipped into dark, new boots.

Or sleep in one another's arms at ten o'clock
on a Saturday in June? — that

smiling child hiding behind
the heavy curtain of a photo booth.

All our daysleep, my love, remember sleep

like brides in violets. Sleep
like sleepy pilots casting

the shadows of their silver jets
onto the silver sailboats
they also sailed
on oceans miles below.

Such nothingness, on the other

side of which
infinity slid
into eternity, insisting

that we had lived together forever — and did.

Index of Titles

Acknowledgments

I would like to thank the following presses and their editors, who supported the publication of the books from which are reprinted sections of this collection:

NYU Press: *Wild Brides*

Carnegie Mellon University Press: *Housekeeping in a Dream* and *What It Wasn't*

Alice James Books: *Fire & Flower*

University of Massachusetts Press: *Dance and Disappear*

Ausable Press: *Gardening in the Dark* and *Lilies Without*

Copper Canyon Press: *Space, in Chains* and *The Infinitesimals*

I am also grateful to the following journals, in which new poems from this collection first appeared:

Alaska Quarterly Review: "On the Properties of Summer"

Arroyo Literary Review: "The Breath"

Ghost Town: "Pandora's Cellar"

The Hampden-Sydney Poetry Review: "In the Meantime"

The Iowa Review: "The Hourglass," "Envelope Addressed to Me with Your Return Address"

Kenyon Review: "The Whole," "For the Return of the Bee,"

Lake Effect: "Praying Mantis in My Husband's Salad"

The Literati Quarterly: "Bored Girl Spits into an Abyss"

New England Review: "The Owls," "Green"

New Republic: "The Enormous Cage"

Plume: "The Face"

Poem-a-Day, Academy of American Poets: "Champagne"

Poetry: "Two Men & a Truck," "The Wall"

The Southern Review: "The Names of the Trees"

Willow Springs: "Spies," "Sensual Pleasures"

"House to House" and "Daysleep" originally appeared in *House to House,* a chapbook published by Likewise Books.

I owe a great debt to the many editors who helped me with these poems and published them along the way. In particular I would like to thank Chase Twichell, C. Dale Young, David Baker, George Looney, Kylan Rice, Don Share, and Christian Wiman.

For crucial advice (about this collection in particular, and my poetry in general), which was offered with tact & grace & at decisive moments, I would like to thank Steph Burt, James Harms, and Tony Hoagland.

For all manner of support, I would like to thank the University of Michigan's English Department (particularly Sidonie Smith and David Porter), the Helen Zell Writers' Program (particularly Linda Gregerson, Tung-Hui Hu, and Khaled Mattawa), and the Residential College (particularly Laura Thomas, Warren Hecht, and Ken Mikolowski).

For being my first, best reader, as well as the love of my life: my husband, Bill Abernethy: *always.*

For love, and for subject matter, and for laughter: my son, Jack Abernethy: *always.*

For love and near-hourly life support for a quarter of a century, my dearest friend and favorite writer, Antonya Nelson.

For kindness, laughter, and friendship that has helped me to live and to write more happily over the last couple of years: Douglas Trevor.

For providing all manner of inspiration, affection, fun times, and support: Andrea Beauchamp, Lucy Eazer, Tarfia Faizullah, and Carrie Wilson.

For her stunning images, specifically the one on the cover of this book, I would like to thank Natacha Nikouline.

For hand-holding and cheerful assistance, Tonaya Craft.

And, of course, I offer my eternal gratitude to Michael Wiegers, whose sustaining presence and encouragement has not only made this book possible, but has also supported, tirelessly, the writing and reading of poetry in general — for me and for so many others—over the last many years.

A FEW NOTES ON POEMS

"Miss Post-Apocalypse" was in part inspired by the story "Where Are You Going, Where Have You Been?" by Joyce Carol Oates.

"Spontaneous Human Combustion: An Introduction" and "Spontaneous Human Combustion: 'Girl, Kissing, Bursts into Flames'" were inspired by the book *Spontaneous Human Combustion,* by Jenny Randles and Peter Hough.

"Guide to Imaginary Places: X-Ray," "Guide to Imaginary Places: Back of the North Wind," and "Guide to Imaginary Places: Abaton" were inspired by Alberto Manguel and Gianni Guadalupi's *Dictionary of Imaginary Places.*

"The Visibility of Spirits" opens with a quotation from *Experience with the Supernatural in Early Christian Times,* by Shirley Jackson Case.

"The Cause of All My Suffering" was inspired by Charles Baudelaire's "One

O'Clock in the Morning," from *Paris Spleen.*

More poems than I can name were inspired by the writings of Richard Grossinger, particularly *The Night Sky* and *Embryogenesis.*

Many of the titles, section titles, and poems' subjects in *The Infinitesimals* were taken from and/or inspired by the Metropolitan Museum of Art's facsimile of *The Cloisters Apocalypse,* and from Jeffrey M. Hoffeld's commentary of the pages of the facsimile.

PREVIOUS PUBLICATION CREDITS

Poems from *Wild Brides* are copyright 1992 by Laura Kasischke. Used with the permission of NYU Press, www.nyupress.org.

Poems from *Housekeeping in a Dream* are copyright 1995 by Laura Kasischke. Used with the permission of Carnegie Mellon University Press, www.cmu.edu/universitypress.

Poems from *Fire & Flower* are copyright 1998 by Laura Kasischke. Used with the permission of Alice James Books, www.alicejamesbooks.org.

Poems from *What It Wasn't* are copyright 2002 by Laura Kasischke. Used with the permission of Carnegie Mellon University Press, www.cmu.edu/universitypress.

Poems from *Dance and Disappear* are copyright 2002 by Laura Kasischke. Used with the permission of the University of Massachusetts Press, www.umass.edu/umpress.

About the Author

Laura Kasischke has published eleven poetry collections and eleven works of fiction. She has been the recipient of the National Book Critics Circle Award for poetry, a Guggenheim Fellowship, and the University of North Texas Rilke Prize, among many other prizes in the U.S. and abroad. Her writing has been translated widely, and three of her novels have been made into films. She lives in Chelsea, Michigan, with her husband and son, and teaches in the Residential College and in the Helen Zell Writers' Program at the University of Michigan.

Poetry is vital to language and living. Since 1972, Copper Canyon Press has published extraordinary poetry from around the world to engage the imaginations and intellects of readers, writers, booksellers, librarians, teachers, students, and donors.

WE ARE GRATEFUL FOR THE MAJOR SUPPORT PROVIDED BY:

THE PAUL G. ALLEN
FAMILY FOUNDATION

amazon *literary*
partnership

4
CULTURE

Anonymous
Jill Baker and Jeffrey Bishop
Anne and Geoffrey Barker
In honor of Ida Bauer, Betsy Gifford, and Beverly Sachar
Donna and Matthew Bellew
Will Blythe
John Branch
Diana Broze
John R. Cahill
Sarah Cavanaugh
The Beatrice R. and Joseph A. Coleman Foundation Inc.
The Currie Family Fund
Stephanie Ellis-Smith and Douglas Smith
Austin Evans
Saramel Evans
Mimi Gardner Gates
Gull Industries Inc. on behalf of William True
The Trust of Warren A. Gummow
William R. Hearst, III
Carolyn and Robert Hedin
Bruce Kahn
Phil Kovacevich and Eric Wechsler

TO LEARN MORE ABOUT UNDERWRITING
COPPER CANYON PRESS TITLES,
PLEASE CALL 360-385-4925 EXT. 103

WE ARE GRATEFUL FOR THE MAJOR SUPPORT PROVIDED BY:

Lakeside Industries Inc. on behalf of Jeanne Marie Lee
Maureen Lee and Mark Busto
Peter Lewis and Johnna Turiano
Ellie Mathews and Carl Youngmann as The North Press
Larry Mawby and Lois Bahle
Hank and Liesel Meijer
Jack Nicholson
Gregg Orr
Petunia Charitable Fund and adviser Elizabeth Hebert
Suzanne Rapp and Mark Hamilton
Adam and Lynn Rauch
Emily and Dan Raymond
Joseph C. Roberts
Jill and Bill Ruckelshaus
Cynthia Sears
Kim and Jeff Seely
Joan F. Woods
Barbara and Charles Wright
Caleb Young as C. Young Creative
The dedicated interns and faithful volunteers
of Copper Canyon Press

The Chinese character for poetry is made up of two parts: "word" and "temple."
It also serves as pressmark for Copper Canyon Press.

This book is set in Whitman, designed by Kent Lew.
The headings are set in Legato, designed by Evert Bloemsma.
Book design by VJB/Scribe. Printed on archival-quality paper.